There is no denying it;  has brought the problem done his homework. Thi wider. It is informative ᴜ many a myth I naively held for truth. Daniel has a passionate heart for love, and I walk away better for having read the work.

—GREG ALLEN
AUTHOR, PRESIDENT, AND FOUNDER
BUILDER OF THE SPIRIT MINISTRIES

The name Daniel Vassell Sr. conjures up sterling memories of a dynamic orator on the frontline subject of love and marriage. Endorsing this book is such a pleasure as the author—prolific and real—expounds the scriptural and fundamental issue that needs bold, uncompromising exposure.

The exhaustive research and very acceptable, open-hearted, and frank discussion uncovers the passionate convictions of a warm "family man." A more devoted and deep straight talk is difficult to find.

May this thoroughly researched and professionally presented ideal offer solace to a loveless society and reignite love in marriage. The promulgation of family values in society is imperative and urgent. Please read on and promote.

—EMMANUEL JOSEPH MOODLEY
SENIOR PASTOR,
BETHSAIDA INTERNATIONAL MINISTRIES
DURBAN, SOUTH AFRICA

*The Love Factor in Marriage* has been written with great concern for today's marriages and families. Daniel Vassell has written with a burden to see marriages and families come under the rule of God's love. With caring insight, the author has presented from his years of experience ministering with couples and families the need to follow the rule of God's love in the home.

—DR. OLIVER MCMAHAN
DEAN OF MINISTRIES
CHURCH OF GOD THEOLOGICAL SEMINARY

Daniel Vassell is an example of one who has learned the meaning of love (unconditional, positive regards). He has shown this through his relationship with Jenny, James, Aleah, his God, and his church. Based on this background, I have looked forward to the completion of *The Love Factor in Marriage*. You will enjoy this book.

—Dr. G. Dennis McGuire
General Overseer
Church of God International Offices

Daniel Vassell has a heart for God and church. However, his zeal for spiritual things does not surpass his zeal for his family. It is evident that he understands that his relationship with his wife will greatly impact his relationship with his children, as well as with God. He is a dedicated student and has worked diligently to prepare a manuscript to relate his findings regarding the establishment of a godly foundation of love in the family relationship. I commend him for his effort to influence a society full of dysfunctional families. We must help the church to realize that before the church was instituted God created the family. Now, we must do all we can to save it!

—John D. Childers
Administrative bishop
Church of God
Northern Ohio

*The Love Factor in Marriage* can help you and your spouse beat the odds of divorce and master the essential principles that make a successful marriage. An excellent resource for pastors and a must for couples.

—Dr. John T. Ramos
Doctor of Ministry in Marriage and Family

Daniel Vassell's *The Love Factor in Marriage* communicates that Jesus' love for the church is the pattern God set for the marital love relationship. This book challenges husbands to love their wives as colaborers and equal partners, to recognize them as "gifts," not as possessions. The indwelling presence of God will supply the needed love for all couples to find complete fulfillment and happiness in marriage and repair any broken pieces of your relationship regardless of circumstances. Not just another book on marriage, this has practical ideas for expanding the love factor in your marriage.

—Dr. Daniel Boling
Administrative Bishop
Church of God
West Virginia

In a day when marriage is under attack, Daniel Vassell offers his heart in addressing the foundation of the marital relationship. *The Love Factor in Marriage* reasserts a biblical view of love and thereby reminds all of us of its power to restore and renew marriage.

—John Kie Vining, D. Min.
International Director of Family Ministry

Daniel J. Vassell Sr. has brought to focus an up-to-date twenty-first century freshness of the love principle that is so vital in the marital affinity. *The Love Factor in Marriage* does raise one's consciousness. The provocative thought principles, ideas, and practicalities are worth being inwardly digested and demonstrated.

He etymologized the word *love*, and vividly declares that "love is knowledge, service, and commitment."

The affirmation of women can be clearly envisioned as a positive note, while from a negative perspective, abuse is "love's silent killer."

If anyone wants the rewards of love, try his suggested lists of ways a husband and wife can express love to one another.

—Dr. Quan Miller
Senior Pastor, 910 Church of God
Cocoa, Florida

The biblical injunction "husbands, love your wives" is set forth in the text in the most serious manner. It is compared with the relationship between Christ and the church. However, this advice is often slighted because of a lack of careful reflection. In *The Love Factor in Marriage* Bishop Daniel

Vassell Sr. has gently, but firmly, reminded us that God has created us with the ability to love and the capacity to be loved. Consequently we have an obligation to love our partners, and in so doing we achieve our full potential according to God's design. *The Love Factor in Marriage* is a must read for all couples.

—BISHOP WAYNE A. VERNON
SENIOR PASTOR, WORD OF LIFE WORSHIP CENTER
JAMAICA AND THE WEST INDIES

THE

# LOVE
# FACT⊙R IN
# MARRIAGE

## DANIEL J. VASSELL SR.

CREATION
HOUSE
A STRANG COMPANY

THE LOVE FACTOR IN MARRIAGE by Daniel J. Vassell Sr.
Published by Creation House
A Strang Company
600 Rinehart Road
Lake Mary, Florida 32746
www.creationhouse.com

Cover design by Karen Grindley

Library of Congress Control Number: 2004105939
International Standard Book Number: 1-59185-605-1

05 06 07 08 09 — 987654321
Printed in the United States of America

# ACKNOWLEDGMENTS

MANY PEOPLE HAVE assisted me in preparing this book, and I cannot possibly name them all. However, I would be remiss if I did not name a few people who have been important to the creation of this book.

I would like to express appreciation to my pastor, Reverend Devon A. Dixon Sr., his wife, Heather, and the members of the East Chester Church of God in Bronx, New York, who gave me the opportunity to share this book with them in sermon form and for their encouragement to turn the sermon into a book.

Appreciation is extended to Sonia Stone and Shandrika Languely, personal friends, for their help and encouragement in the early draft.

Thanks also to Joycelyn Brown—youth pastor of Driftwood Church of God and an English teacher in Toronto, Canada—for reading this book to see if it addresses the issue of love between husbands and wives and its relationship to youth and children.

Reverend Cauldric Alex, pastor of Cambria Church of God in Boston, Massachusetts—a personal friend and student of the Word—for his help and insights on the abuse of women in the twentieth century.

Dr. Yvonne Johnson—wife of Dr. Raphael Johnson, the pastor of Holy Trinity Parish Church in Cambria Heights, New York—read the manuscript for readability. Dr. Johnson is professor of English at Columbia University in New York.

Thanks to Sophia Morrison, Diana McIntosh, and Julian Nembhard for helping me select appropriate topics.

Special thanks to Creation House Press for publishing this book as a resource for singles and couples who are interested in learning about the love factor in marriage. Thanks especially to Robert Caggiano for his expertise in editing and Karen Grindley for her creative cover design.

And last, but not least, special thanks to Jenny, my loving wife, for working with me through many of the issues addressed in this book. Thank you for the support and encouragement you have given me while I was writing this book. Thank you for believing in me. I love you.

I would like to thank my son, James, and his friend, Hannah, for reading and giving me feedback from the perspective of two youth seeking to know God's will for love in marriage. Your feedback was very valuable and insightful.

I would like to thank the various churches and ministries for the opportunities they gave me.

Whatever the result of this book may be, I give credit to all who offered suggestions, insights, and prayers. If reading this book impacts one or one million lives, their help will have been rewarded.

I especially give honor and praise to God for His guidance, His Word, and His love. Without Him, this book would not have been possible.

# CONTENTS

| | | |
|---|---|---|
| Preface | | xi |
| Foreword | | xii |
| Introduction | | 1 |
| 1 | The Love Factor Ignite | 3 |
| 2 | The Love Bundle | 16 |
| 3 | Ecstasy Restored | 26 |
| 4 | The Loving Thing to Do | 31 |
| 5 | The Missing Factor | 54 |
| 6 | Marriage Glory! | 60 |
| 7 | Loving Partnership | 63 |
| 8 | Silencing Love | 80 |
| 9 | Keeping Love Alive in the Stages of Marriage | 95 |
| 10 | Love and Intimacy | 111 |
| 11 | Love and Sex | 118 |
| 12 | Love's Rewards | 132 |
| 13 | Loving You Forever | 140 |
| | Conclusion | 154 |
| | Notes | 160 |
| | About the Author | 164 |

This book is dedicated to my parents, Evangelists William and Louise Vassell, who loved each other through more than forty-five years of marriage. Their lives exemplified the true biblical love—unconditional agape love—for one another during difficult times as well as happy times.

It is also dedicated to my loving and lovely wife, Jennifer Ann Marie Vernon-Vassell, for her patience and love during our years of marriage. She has, through love and grace, given me time to learn how to love her as Christ requires. This love has taught our children, Daniel J. Vassell Jr. and Jennifer Aleah Vassell, to be obedient and respectful to us as Ephesians 6:1 dictates.

# Preface

I N 1998 MY pastor invited me to speak during the church family month. I sought God for a word, and He gave me the text from Ephesians. As I prepared the sermon, I realized that what the Lord was revealing to me would take more than a forty-minute sermon to convey His message to singles and couples. The people who heard the message encouraged me to do more research on the topic, and because of my findings, this book evolved.

Summing up all that is involved with fulfilling the command to love one's spouse is difficult to put into a single volume. I do not pretend to have all the answers; however, I pray that this text will raise the consciousness of every reader, thus allowing the Holy Spirit to minister in a way that will ultimately bring about concerted reform.

As you read this book, I pray that the Holy Spirit will minister to you as He did to me. May *The Love Factor in Marriage* help married couples successfully face and survive the twenty-first century with God as the head of their families.

For the readers who are single, I trust that *The Love Factor in Marriage* will provide you with some insight and knowledge that will guide you in establishing a relationship based on a godly foundation of love that will enhance your season of marriage when you do enter into it.

# FOREWORD

WE LIVE IN a rapidly changing world. The speed at which our world is changing catches many of us completely unaware, until some revelation or incident reveals how far we have been left behind. Many are frightened by these changing times and retreat into the comfort of past traditions and mind-sets. Others feel threatened by the change in the status quo and resist any changes at all. Unfortunately, the changes caused by the explosion of communication, technology, and knowledge have affected the family, in general, and marital relationships, in particular.

However, in the midst of this change, there are some absolutes. Daniel Vassell has identified one of these absolutes in writing *The Love Factor in Marriage*. After years of ministry to couples and singles, his burden for marriages and the marital relationship has prompted him to once again call Christians to love their spouses as the Bible demands. Writing primarily from the man's perspective, Daniel insists that a man should not let his love for his wife be determined by what Hollywood portrays or by the actions of those in contemporary society. There is clear biblical instruction regarding how a man is to treat his wife.

*The Love Factor in Marriage* can serve as a valuable resource to pastors, couples, and singles who are anticipating marriage. It gives clear biblical instruction, valuable insight, and practical suggestions for keeping love the vital factor in the marital relationship.

—DR. R. LAMAR VEST
(FORMER) INTERNATIONAL PRESIDING BISHOP, CHURCH OF GOD,
CLEVELAND, TN

# INTRODUCTION

WHEN I BEGAN writing this book, my intention was to write a resource manual that would be beneficial to couples who are experiencing difficulties in their marriages and provide a resource for those planning on entering the holy estate of marriage. I quickly found that it would not only be a resource for troubled marriages, but also a timely resource for all marriages that have the intention of maximizing the power of love available to their union.

I researched many different areas that would or could affect the marriage relationship and found that abuse and love junkies are creating havoc in many marriages. I discovered that many single-parent families are caused by divorce. I learned that many marriages are in trouble because couples are not able to communicate with each other through their love language.

Another major discovery was that there is a war going on over what constitutes a marriage. There is a war waging in the judiciary and political systems waging to redefine the marriage union to include same-sex union.

The greatest discovery was that there are many marriages not experiencing the fulfillment of love as the couples hoped for. Many of these couples claim to be Christians, a religion that is built upon love.

And not so recently, because of the terrorists' actions on September 11, 2001, it became evident that if we do not find a way to help married couples bond and become closer—to speak the same love language—marriages will continue to fail. With the anxiety that terrorism has caused us, families need each other

1

for comfort support. And if they are not letting God be their guide, marriages will crumble.

God has given us guidelines and principles for good marriages to grow and mature in love. He has created our bodies to function in love starting with romance ignited by phenylethylamine (PEA) to reality love sustained through oxytocin (OKC-see-TOE-sun).

God has not only created us to function in love by His natural order, but He also has given us the Holy Spirit and His Word as the adhesives that will hold marriages together. The Holy Spirit is the Spirit of love. (See 1 John 4:8, 16.) When He is operating in us, He gives us the fruit of the spirit (see Galatians 5:22) that will cause our love to grow and mature.

God has created men to be the conduit or channel of love for marriage, and women are built to give love in response to what they receive. When husbands and wives submit to the design of God for their marriage, their love grows stronger and sweeter over time, even in difficult times. Couples whose love lives are anchored in unconditional love are able to surmount life's difficulties and challenges because of the Holy Spirit's presence and help. They find greater rewards in being faithful.

God does not abandon couples after the honeymoon is over as some would think. He is ever present to help couples grow in love as they go through the various stages of marriage. When love is operating as an integral part of the marriage relationship, couples will experience greater health, longer life, and better welfare than those living without love.

To get the full benefits of *The Love Factor in Marriage*, couples must follow God's direction, depend on Him, and ask for His daily leadership so they can have godly marriages—marriages that stand the test of time.

In order for a marriage to stand that test of time "a man will leave his father and mother and be joined to his wife, and the two will become one flesh. This is a great mystery, and I am applying it to Christ and the church. Each of you, however, should love his wife as himself, and a wife should respect her husband" (Eph. 5:31–33).

This is the hallmark and foundation upon which *The Love Factor in Marriage* is based. Now let us delve into the mystery-love factor.

*Chapter 1*

# THE LOVE FACTOR IGNITE

Husbands, love your wives, just as Christ also loved the church, and gave himself for her.

—EPHESIANS 5:25

TINA TURNER, HAVING been abused and abandoned emotionally by her husband, wrote a song entitled, "What's Love Got To Do With It." In the song she reveals a sad story about love and marriage. Tina sang, love was, "but a second-hand emotion." My answer to Tina is, no, love is not a second hand emotion. It is the lifeblood of Christian marriages and the church.

John 13:34 tells us, "A new command I give you: love one another. As I have loved you, so you must love one another." This text declares the Christian community is a loving community, and those living in the community must practice pure love in their marriages.

Today, there is a major problem in secular culture and the Christian community concerning the value of love in marriage. More emphasis is placed on the feelings of love rather than the choice to love in marriage. Many marriages have failed because couples claim their feelings of love died in the relationship. When love feelings fail, many couples become discouraged and disillusioned in their relationships. They waver or simply give up.

I have often heard the saying, "Marriages are made in heaven, but they are lived out on earth." How true! Marriage is a divine institution, designed for the good of human existence on earth. It is perfect in design and wholesome as is. The problem with many married couples is they enter marriage without the proper knowledge of marriage, lack of adequate preparation, faulty understanding of love, and poor commitment dynamics. Other couples enter marriage with a wounded self-image or unnecessary baggage.

3

The problem is not marriage; it is people! Rather than fixing the "people" problem of marriage, many experts are determined to redefine it. The only person who can change the marriage institution is God.

It is time for the silent majority to rise in support of the marriage institution before a small group of people redefines the law as happened in Canada. The decision to change the marriage status was not done by the people of Canada; it was done by a handful of judges and legislators.

Marriage is a union between a man and a woman, but today the gay and lesbian groups in society are trying to redefine the law of marriage to include same sex-unions. God established the marriage institution, and no law will nullify God's law. In God's court of justice, the marriage union is not up for debate.

The Creator of the universe established marriage for heterosexual relationships between a man and woman as outlined in Genesis 1:27–28; 2:18, 23–24. All throughout history, humanity has accepted that norm. Today, Canada, Belgium, and the Netherlands have legalized same-sex marriage. The United States of America and many other countries are fighting the battle in their courts to redefine the marriage code. The day same sex marriage is legalized in other countries, the Pandora's box of all sexual immoralities will be opened. There will be no limit to how far humans will go to degrade themselves in sexually debauchery. The help society needs is a program for couples to live their lives in love.

The traditional marriage, as we know it, is a challenging experience for many couples. In fact, marriage, whether by choice or arranged, is under attack. The devil is bent on destroying the backbone of society, but we cannot allow him to destroy God's gift to humanity.

God designed marriage to be a place where each person in the relationship could grow and be a healing agent of love.

The love problem in marriage is a twentieth-century phenomenon. In our early history, people entered marriage based on choice or arrangement usually made by parents or the church. In his book *Keeping the Love You Find* Dr. Harville Hendrix, PhD said:

The combination of love and marriage is a phenomenon of very recent history—and it is a volatile mix. Marriages were arranged. Marriages were typically passionless, but stable; their primary agenda was the continuity of the family and community, the perpetuation of property rights. *Only* infrequently, and usually accidentally, was romantic love connected with the marriage partner.[1]

He further said:

With the emergence of democracy in America and the destruction of the monarchic system in England and France, these political changes brought with them the emergence of the idea that the individual could decide his destiny. The rights of the individual came to include the right to marry the person of one's choice, thus radically transforming marriage from a sociopolitical institution to a psychological and spiritual process. For the first time in history, the energy of attraction between men and women was directed into and contained within the structure of marriage.[2]

Even though marriages occur through individual choices of their partners, Dr. Hendrix believes:

There is still some kind of parallel to the arranged marriage, in the sense that as the arranged marriage had a specific purpose, so our unconscious selects a partner to suit its particular needs.[3]

It is true couples marry for love, and romantic fulfillment in marriage is expected. However, Dr. Hendrix further adds:

What is going on in mate selection is not love, but need. Love, if it appears at all, appears in marriage, as a result of our commitment to healing our partner. Individuals choose an imago partner in order to grow and heal.[4]

Today, many couples in the Western world enter marriage based on the primary feelings of romantic love. They fail to understand they entered the union more out of choice and commitment to love than feelings.

Love is a choice. It is action and service. According to Dr. Hendrix:

> Throughout history, mankind has deemed the heart the center of love, but scientists tell us love is in the mind and it is fueled by chemicals and chemistry.[5]

Scripture suggests love begins in the mind—it did so long before scientists could discover it as fact. The apostle Paul, led by the Holy Spirit, commanded husbands to "love your wives, just as Christ loved the church and gave himself up for her" (Eph. 5:25). It is clear, from this scripture, he was calling upon husbands to make a choice consciously to love their wives. One cannot command a feeling. Feelings follow actions.

The word *love* in this context is a verb. Through Paul, God is telling husbands to make the choice to love their wives and demonstrate it through loving action, and service as illustrated by Jesus in Ephesians 5:25–31. When husbands and wives make the choice to love and demonstrate their choice with loving actions or service, the feelings of love will always follow.

Many couples have given up on their marriage because of a lack of feeling loved. They claim they are no longer in love with each other, that their love is dead. Hence, they choose divorce as a way out of a loveless relationship so they can move on to another relationship. According to statistics, over 75 percent of those second marriages will end in divorce as well.

Divorce may allow people to escape bad marriages, but until couples take steps to guarantee good marriages, to facilitate individual happiness and fulfillment, and to learn what they are about, they will continue to have joyless marriages and troubled children. Society will become more dysfunctional by the decade. Divorce is not the answer to a loveless marriage. Love is the answer.

Couples who make the choice to end their marriage on the grounds their love is dead fail to understand their love was not dead; it was just wounded. Getting a new spouse will not change the reason why love died in the first marriage; the problem will simply flow over into the next marriage. What is needed is a mental and spiritual change, followed by an emotional change. One of the major problems with married couples is they are socialized love-lust junkies. As a result, they are not able to function in a normal marital relationship.

A stable marital relationship is one characterized by a couple that understands love is something you do; it is not something you get "right." It is a mystery to be lived, not a problem to be solved. Love junkies cannot understand the hardest truth about marriage. Dr. Hendrix said:

> The hard truth of the matter is that in order to have a healing marriage, we must change and become the kind of person that our partner needs in order to heal. The changes required of us in order to become healing partners for our mates are often the changes that are most difficult for us to make.[6]

The love-lust junkie relationship is built on romantic love, lust, or infatuation that is usually short-lived. Once the infatuation or romantic love bubble bursts, the marriage relationship begins to wane. Love junkies do not understand romantic love is a time bomb; it carries seeds of destruction. The romantic love stage in marriage is supposed to end so real love can build the relationship. Real love is something entirely different—better—but it only comes to couples that wrestle with their problems and weather the course.

When romantic love moves to caring love, the relationship will move beyond feelings and will become one in which partners can begin to express genuine concern for each other's welfare. This deep intimacy will evolve into real love.

Romantic love usually lasts for a few weeks or a few years; however, give it time and the bubble will burst. The veil of illusion will be lifted, and Love junkies will see the disappointing truth of their partners. The romantic-love stage in a love junky relationship is one buoyed by hope and endorphins. Each partner is voluntarily providing what the other wants and needs. It creates a false view of reality. There is a false sense of expectation filled with anticipation that the relationship will be fulfilling. However, once the marital commitment is made—often the wedding ceremony changes that—all agony breaks loose. Anticipation becomes expectation, and both partners tend to extract some of the unconditional giving that characterizes an early relationship. At the same time, they begin to demand or feel entitled to have their own needs met.

Some love junkie couples stay in the marriage to heal each other. Others leave the relationship and go back to the singles' world to search for another to produce the love-lust chemistry. I believe the divorce rate is high in the church community today because many of those couples were love junkies themselves.

Many psychologists label the above description as, "love junkies or lust junkies." A love junkie is a person who is "addicted to relationship highs." The love junkie phenomenon became a major issue when changes took place in the dating game. In the early days of American history, parents regulated dating with the support of the church and community. Today, generally speaking, individuals are allowed to start dating as early as they choose. Many children are beginning to date early, with parental support, without limits or boundary.

With little or no boundaries, individuals are left up to their own judgments and consciences to determine what to do or not to do on dates. The freedom to date at an early age, without proper limits or boundary, has helped create a love-junkie era. Many cannot count the number of relationships they have had. Many of those relationships were short-lived for many reasons. The reason those relationships were short-lived is their dates did not supply the emotional need. Hence, they move on to another relationship. The sad part of the story is many of those relationships included premarital sex, which makes the love junkie problem much more complicated. People with multiple relationships have not learned what it is to be committed. As a result, after they get married, divorce is likely. Then they move on to another relationship.

In her book *Anatomy of Love,* Helen Fisher stated that the love-lust junkie relationships last only about four years. In her opinion,

"The infatuation and romantic love lasts only to lengthen the male-female partnership long enough for procreation."[7]

According to Barbara DeAngelis, PhD, in her book *Are You the One for Me?*:

> These people are often addicted to the instant high of infatuation. They want those firecrackers popping and rockets going off. But the high of lust-love-at-first-sight is often followed by the low of disappointment you feel when the relationship does not turn out the way you hoped it would. So many people get rid of the mate-lover, but then keep the problem and take it right to that next person who produces the right chemistry.[8]

The love-lust junkies also have another problem. They crave the intoxication of chemistry and infatuation. When their bodies build up a tolerance to those chemical reactions, it takes more and more chemistry to bring about that special feeling of love. Barbara DeAngelis goes on to say:

> Many adults go through life in a series of six-month, to three or four year relationships. Some do this even if they are married. In fact, if these Love Junkies stay married, they are quite likely to seek affairs to fuel their chemical highs.[9]

Love junkie is not a new phenomenon. It has been around for years. The problem is that it is becoming popular and the norm for life today. I would like to take a look at two stories—one from the Old Testament and another from the New Testament. They both reveal love junkie relationships.

## SCANDALOUS LOVE

Many marriages are hurting today because one partner is not living according to the marriage vows. Other marriages are filled with infidelity, separation and isolation. Partners are living as friends rather than husband and wife. Those marriages are suffering because one or both people are love lust junkies. Is there any help or hope?

The story of Hosea and Gomer reveal the rippling effects of a love junkie caught in a scandalous love story. Hosea, a prophet of God, married a woman who was a prostitute. (See Hosea 3:1.) Marrying a prostitute was considered a tragedy according to Jewish teachings, but the prophet obeyed God and married Gomer. Like all husbands, Hosea was expecting his wife to remain faithful to him once they were married. However, that was not the case. Like many blind lovers, Hosea might have believed the marriage would have changed Gomer or stopped her from having any other immoral relationships. That was not the case. Unresolved premarital problems will not be solved by marriage. Relational baggage must be dealt with before anyone enters into marriage, whether one is a Christian or not.

Gomer's lifestyle before and during her marriage reveals a classic example of a love-lust junkie. She could not be satisfied with one relationship. Hence, she left her marital union and went after other men to satisfy her emotional and love-lust needs.

Without a miracle of God or marriage therapy, a love junkie cannot change their own behavior.

A careful reading of Hosea 3:1 would show that Hosea did not sit back and allow Gomer to stray without resisting her. As a loving husband, he made various attempts to get her to change her lifestyle and come back home to him after she left him. However, she refused. Whenever unconditional love exists in a marriage, God will show up to deliver. Hosea tried to get his wife to return home, then the Lord intervened in Hosea 3:1. He said, "Go show love again," bring your wife, Gomer, back to your matrimonial home and life. God sent Hosea when He realized Gomer was ready.

Hosea was told to love Gomer with a special kind of love. The love God commanded Hosea to demonstrate toward Gomer was unconditional, selfless and redeeming love. Hosea was to love Gomer as the Lord loved Israel. Such love is not expressed in feelings or words but in redeeming actions.

The key idea in unconditional or redeeming love is choosing to do good even when the desired response is not reciprocated.

Unconditional or redeeming love expresses itself in establishing and maintaining a loving relationship even when the beneficiary does not deserve that love. The only way Hosea could get Gomer back was to obey God's command and give her unconditional love.

Hosea continued to love unfaithful Gomer just as the Lord, Israel's Husband, continued to love unfaithful Israel. Gomer was immersed in unfaithfulness to her husband, which hurt him emotionally. But because Hosea was saturated with the Spirit of God, his love toward her did not die. It was wounded but not dead. The text addressed Hosea as a friend. The word *friend* suggests Hosea still had some feelings toward her.

It is also important to note Gomer is called *a woman*, not *wife*. *A woman* would describe the state of separation in which she was living.

Hosea was willing to do anything to redeem his woman and restore her to her wifely role and responsibility. In his search for her, he found Gomer for sale in the slave market and bought her back.

Imagine how Hosea must have felt when he found Gomer. She broke his heart and decimated their family. She disgraced herself and him. She was now the degraded property of another man. But, he chose to obey God's command to "go again and love" her regardless of his feelings.

Obeying God's command cost Hosea much. He purchased Gomer for the price of a slave, but it appears Hosea had to scrape the bottom of his financial barrel to raise the redemption price.

Hosea bought Gomer back physically, but it would take time to restore the emotional connections. Gomer came back to the marriage with unresolved issues, and Hosea decided he would deal with the problems that existed in the marriage.

To address the problem, Hosea placed Gomer in a therapeutic setting in which she would have time to understand and appreciate then respond in kind to his unconditional and redeeming love. The therapy was that he would have regard for her as a child of God and respect her. He would watch over her and be kindly disposed toward her. His affections, interests, and thoughts would be directed toward her.

The therapeutic setting and the requirements he arranged for Gomer and himself provided the necessary ingredients for healing and restoration. Hosea's therapeutic process included three disciplines under which he and Gomer would live for a period of time.

1. She would not go after other lovers. She would cease, stop, and avoid any contact with all other male friends. Instead, she would abide at home, devoted to household duties and shut-off from would-be lovers. "With me," means Gomer would live with Hosea in their home and be solely for him.

2. She would not have sexual relations with any man, including her husband.

3. Hosea would have no connection with any other woman but would keep himself exclusively for Gomer. Hosea would wait until she was fully delivered from the desires and passions of strange relationships with other men.

The therapy took an indefinite and relatively long period of time but not forever. The therapy was over when Gomer's desires and passions returned to her husband, and she became addicted to him in such a way that she pursued him with fear and respect. With the return of fidelity, Hosea and Gomer experienced a rewarding time of bliss in their marriage.

Scripture does not describe how Gomer responded to Hosea's actions. But the description of the ultimate victory of God's love for Israel in verses 4–5 implies Hosea's personal victory in his redemptive actions toward Gomer. After the therapy of "many days," Gomer returned to love Hosea as the Israelites would "return and seek the Lord their God and David their king."

Gomer would tremble in amazement at the power and goodness of the love demonstrated by Hosea for her—the same way Israel would "come trembling to the Lord" for "His blessings in the last days" (Hos. 3:5).

The Hosea and Gomer scandalous love story typifies a particular love junkie relationship. In the midst of the crisis, the husband experienced the baptism of the Holy Spirit. Then he received the power to love his wife unconditionally. When he responded to his love junkie wife with unconditional love and applied the above three steps, his marriage was restored from the rippling effects of infidelity and pain.

## A LYING LOVER

In the fourth chapter of the Book of John we meet a love junkie named Mary who had serial relationships. Jesus asked Mary to call her husband. She replied, "I have no husband." Jesus said, "You are right when you say you have no husband. The fact is, you have had five husbands, and the man you now have is not your husband. What you have just said is quite true" (John 4:17–18).

Love junkies are not usually able to see the truth about their lifestyles. Mary could not see she was at fault and needed help. Her problem was men were not meeting her needs and she thought that by changing partners one day she would find "Mr. Right." Mary declared, "I have no husband." What Mary was really saying was, "I am in a relationship, but my emotional needs are not being met. So as soon as I find another Mr. Right, who will supply my emotional needs, I am gone."

Jesus read her life and told her she was lying. He said, "The fact is, you have had five husbands, and the man you now have is not your husband."

Mary was living with a man, but she was not actually married to him, so she did not consider herself married. But the word of the Lord says, "What? know ye not that he which is joined to an harlot is one body? for two, saith he, shall be one flesh" (1 Cor. 6:16, KJV). Jesus opened Mary's eyes when He told her about the love-lust junkie lifestyle she was living. She declared, "Sir, I perceive that thou art a prophet" (John 4:19, KJV).

Once Mary surrendered her life to Jesus Christ, and accepted the Holy Spirit in her life, she was delivered from her love junkie lifestyle. Then she was transformed into an ambassador of Jesus Christ declaring the power of God when she said, "Come, see a man who told me everything I ever did: Could this be the Christ? They came out of the town and made their way toward way him" (John 4:29–30).

Before I go any further, let me speak to you. If you are a love junkie, or you know someone who is a love junkie, there is a cure.

The solution to the love-lust junkie relationship is to receive a spiritual transformation that comes with the indwelling and infilling of the Holy Spirit. What brought the change in Mary's life was the infilling of the Holy Spirit who provided agape love. It took place after Mary said, "Sir, give me this water so that I will not get thirsty and have to keep coming here to draw water" (John 4:15). What she received was a spiritual cleansing and the indwelling presence of the God of love who transformed her life and made her a living testimony.

The Holy Spirit broke the love junkie Spirit and replaced it with agape love. That is the foundation upon which all other love is built. Agape love is unconditional love. It aims your focus on the needs of your spouse, not yours alone.

When God made man, He blew the breath of life into his lungs and deposited agape love. It was agape love that kept Adam and Eve together before and after the fall. Agape love is God's permanent glue to keep marriages together and healthy. (See Hosea 3:1.) The Holy Spirit is the agent or power God has placed in human hearts to activate, regulate, and maintain love. (See Acts 1:8.)

I am convinced the Holy Spirit will realign chemical imbalances to stop people from pursuing the love-lust junkie lifestyle and cause them to live a lifetime of monogamous unconditional love relationships. However, in order for that healing to take place one must confess to God that they need His help and seek to follow the biblical injunction.

The biblical injunction declares husbands are the ones responsible for love in the marriage relationship. (See Ephesians 5:25.) They are to be the conduit, channel, and custodian of the love life in marriage. It is in unconditionally loving our partners that we make it safe for them to be open to love. Letting that love sink in over time so trust can build, allows their fullness to come back into being so they can feel their oneness and totality. *It* is the love we give that heals our partner, and the love we receive that heals us.

A spirit-filled Christian marriage, built on unconditional love, will always seek to satisfy the other person's love needs on a daily basis. Why? Because each spouse's happiness and healing is the ultimate goal of a loving relationship; and a one-time love event cannot sustain any marriage. It is an ongoing, unconditional exercise. Marital relationship is what God designed for couples to practice and experience intimate love. However, one of the biggest problems with most marriages is that couples are entering in without proper guidance or counsel. As a result, they bring in baggage, unresolved issues, and expectations that will destroy the marriage.

Adam started his relationship with Eve in perfect harmony. His love chemicals were working fine. Sin did not nullify his chemical response to Eve and likewise Eve's to Adam. Sin brought guilt and shame instead. However, they continued to love each other until death.

## DISCUSSION

1. How does marriage help to heal one's inner hurt?

2. How can you build and strengthen your marriage?

3. What is the cause of the love-junkie experience?

4. How can an individual break the love-junkie experience?

5. Why are love-junkie relationships usually short lived?

6. What constitutes a stable relationship?

7. Would you agree Mary was a love junkie? Give reasons for or against.

8. How would you discuss love as action and service in your marriage or relationship?

*Chapter 2*

# THE LOVE BUNDLE

*Husbands ought to love their wives as their own bodies. He who loves his wife loves himself.*

—EPHESIANS 5:28

THE EXALTATION TO love your wife or husband does not mean in feelings only. Love is knowledge, service, and commitment demonstrated in a bundle of ways. In the Greek language, there are five words used to describe love, 1) *agape*, unconditional love; 2) *eros*, romantic love; 3) *phileo*, friendship; 4) *storge*, belonging; and 5) *epithumia*, lovemaking.

These will be my focus as I discuss how husbands and wives are to love each other. The English definition of *love* is limited in scope and range. Therefore, as husbands and wives, we must understand the command to love using the Greek etymology of *love*, not the Greek mythology of love.

The Greek meaning of the word *love,* used in Ephesians 5:25, refers to the love God wants husbands to display toward their wives. Agape love is a selfless love, a giving and sacrificial love. It is the love of the mind and will, as well as the heart. It is not only a love of affection and feelings, but it is also a love of will and commitment. It is the love that works for the highest good even if the person does not deserve to be loved.

Jesus' love for the church is the pattern God set for a husband's love toward his wife. A wife's love for her husband is patterned after the church's love for Christ. When this kind of love is demonstrated, a wife will melt in her husband's arms and willingly accept his loving authority as head of the family. Husbands will be spoilt rotten by the love, respect, and honor they receive.

In a Christian marriage, agape is the foundation upon which all other love must be built. If couples do not base their love for each other on agape love, it will not stand the trials and tests of time. In unconditional love God is saying to the husband, as Christ loves the church so should he love his wife. In return, wives need to cultivate ways to express love to their husbands in response to the love they are receiving. Love must be a two way street. If one spouse is always giving love and the other is taking it without reciprocating, it will lead to frustration and a love-starved relationship. In his book, *Fall in Love and Stay in Love*, Dr. Willard J. Harley Jr. says couples must be "givers and takers" mutually.[1]

Unconditional love is an unselfish love. It is an action you make happen. It is a love you determine to give without performance. You love whether or not the other desires your love. It requires finding out the emotional needs of your partner and fulfilling them. It expects nothing in return; it is a gift. Dr. Hendrix says:

> Unconditional love—or, more accurately, unconditional giving—has not been in vogue in recent times. Too often we tend to think in terms of a balance sheet, of *earning* someone's love, or having him or her earn ours—an *economic* model. Unconditional love sounds like a willingness to love someone no matter what he or she does, even if he or she neglects or abuses us.[2]

Loving your partner unconditionally simply means making a commitment to give them what they need without asking for anything in return— without rendering a bill for service. Instead of, "I will come home earlier if you will have more sex with me," we say, "I will come home earlier because I need to spend more time with you."

Paul did not leave the command for husbands to love their wives to their own interpretations; instead, he elaborated by saying the husband should have the same love for his wife that he has for his own body. (See Ephesians 5:28.) That means the husband must nourish and cherish his wife. The word *nourish* (*ektrephei*) means to feed, clothe, nurture, and look after her until she is mature in the marriage, then continue nourishing her as long as she lives. The word *cherish* (*thalpei*) means to hold within the heart; to treat with warmth, tenderness, care, affection, and appreciation.

A difference would exist in marriages if husbands would just nourish and cherish their wives as they do their own bodies! Think about the meanings of *nourish* and *cherish* for just a moment, then imagine the changes that have taken place or could take place in your marriage.

It is important to note the New Testament provides a great treatise on love. Paul's understanding and discussion of love makes it a central theme in his writing. His use of the noun *agape* makes the term almost a technical one. Before Paul, in fact, the Greek term *agape* was seldom used. Paul took the seldom-used term and filled it with Christian meaning. The love about which Paul wrote is somewhat different from the love we normally experience and speak about.

Christian love is not simply an emotion, which arises because of the character of the one loved, nor is it due to the loving quality of the lover. The love of a child of God is agape love—unconditional love. It is a relationship of self-giving which results from God's activity in Christ. The source of Christian love is God, and the believer's response of faith makes love a human possibility. (See Romans 5:8 and 5:5, respectively.) Agape lays the foundation in which the other types of love can flourish. A marriage that has a foundation built on agape love does not look for a way out of problems but seeks a way to use the problem to provide healing, wholeness, and a building block for love.

*Eros* is presented in our culture as sex. However, in the Greek usage, *eros* refers to romantic love, that which gives you the thrills and sweeps you off your feet. Romantic love bonds lovers together so they will stick around long enough to see if they can make it work. It gives couples the strength for the long undertaking of self-repair and the arduous work of a conscious relationship. When couples are in love, they have the feeling they can do whatever it takes to work things out. Ongoing romantic love in marriage takes a great effort on the couples part to keep it alive.

Here are three action tips to fulfill *eros* love:

1. Think about your partner throughout the day.

2. Think about the romantic moments you have spent with each other.

3. Plan for romance without limit to your imagination— be creative.

Let us take a look at some additional Greek words for love and their meanings.

*Phileo* is friendship or companionate love which produces closeness and companionship. It is to be a best friend, to be fond of an individual, having affection for; denoting personal attachment. It is a time is spent sharing intimate thoughts or reminiscing on whatever comes to mind. It is in this time of sharing that you build closeness, oneness, and a soul bond with your partner. It is in this kind of love that emotional bonds grow. This is one of the most powerful loves. Phileo is the gateway to most love perversion. There are many married couples, but most are not best friends.

Many married couples are living like single people. Their lives are so busy that they have no time for each other. True friends make time for each other. Your spouse should be your best friend.

Today, with the rise of many women working outside the home and the growth of electronic media, many marriages are hurting in their friendship. Many couples are becoming strangers in their relationship. More time is spent outside the home with other people than with the spouse. Many couples are establishing friendship outside their matrimonial home where emotional needs can be met. More and more couples are spending time on the Internet establishing friendship with ghost friends.

Many people find Internet friends to be unintimated, so they feel comfortable sharing their whole intimate soul without fear or shame. The Internet provides an environment that removes the fear and shame many people have while discussing personal and intimate issues. As a result of the privacy gained through the electronic media, there have been many friendships established outside the matrimonial relationship that are experiencing emotional adultery.

How do you know if your friendship is on the verge of emotional adultery? When you begin to discuss your spouse's personal and intimate problems and issues without fear or concern you are opening the gate to emotional adultery, which will lead to full adultery. Guard your marriage by building a friendship with your spouse and be sure to share all your feelings and thoughts together.

*Storge* is the feeling of belonging and security. A wife is most happy when she feels secure in her husband's love, loyalty, and trust. By complimenting and praising your spouse instead of being critical, by proving your loyalty by being supportive and by offering encouraging and romantic words, you can give your spouse a sense of belonging. A husband feels as if belongs when his wife makes him feel significant, that her life would be incomplete without him and that he is the one who makes her feel complete and fulfilled. When husbands and wives feel a sense of belonging, they are secure in significance. They will be able to build an emotional bond that is impregnable.

*Epithumia* is "lovemaking," an art that develops with time. One of the problems with *epithumia* love is many individuals enter into a marriage relationship with the wrong concept of lovemaking. The view many couples have of lovemaking is determined by their premarital experiences; those false, slow-motion choreographed movie scenes; fairytales; and imaginations of big boys' or big girls' stories.

As a result of faulty expectations, many husbands and wives struggle in the art of lovemaking. The Bible does not provide much detail on lovemaking and techniques, but it addresses the marriage rights in Exodus 21:10, erotic caresses in Song of Solomon 2:6; 7:1–9, fondling in Genesis 26:8, and pleasure in conceiving in Genesis 18:12. Yet, these are set forth in the context of the behavior of married couples.

Intimate sexual behavior outside of marriage is considered sexual immorality from the biblical perspective. The Bible discusses sex as a gift from God, and it leaves the details of lovemaking up to the married couple. Lovemaking techniques should be discussed by the married couple, and the decisions should please each spouse as it provides pleasure and fulfillment.

The Song of Solomon celebrates God's gift of bodily love

between man and woman as it is portrayed in Genesis 2:23–25. In that passage, the Creator's wisdom and bounty are displayed. So, husbands and wives, do not be bashful! Our Creator designed lovemaking for pleasure and procreation.

I will discuss sex in more detail in a later chapter. Until I do, here are four simple suggestions to enjoy *epithumia*. God created us as sexual beings, and we all have needs for fulfillment.

1. It is appropriate to think "sexy" about your spouse.

2. Focus on the joy and pleasure of lovemaking. However, there will be times when your desire for lovemaking will not be mutual.

3. Discuss the issue with your spouse and reach a compromise; thus, both will be fulfilled.

4. Discuss the likes and dislikes of lovemaking with your spouse. Read books on techniques, and be creative! Become a 24-hour lover. It takes time to set the pace and create the environment so each partner can savor the ambiance.

Husbands and wives must take time to utilize and master one of the most powerful and greatest gifts of life—love. It is a wonderful gift that produces an ecstatic experience.

In the Old Testament we find Solomon, in his biblical wisdom, talking about love: "Love is as strong as death…Many waters cannot quench love.…If one were to give all the wealth of his house for love, it would be utterly scorned" (Song of Sol. 8:6–7, author's paraphrase). Solomon also indicated there is a right time and place for love when he said, "Daughters of Jerusalem, I charge you…do not arouse or awaken love until it so desires" (Song of Sol. 3:5). In these poems, love is portrayed in its power, splendor, freshness, and devotion for others. Love takes many forms—moments of union and separation, ecstasy and anguish, longing and fulfillment.

Study the Book of Song of Solomon. Couples in love need to look carefully at Song of Solomon to obtain lessons on how to love each other. The following love themes will reveal so much to you about love that it will add spice to your love life:

- Longing is a part of love (1:1–8).
- Love will not be silent (1:9–2:7).
- Spring and love go together (2:8–17).
- Love is exclusive (3:1–5).
- Love is enhanced by friendship (3:6–11).
- Love sees only the beautiful (4:1–7).
- Love involves giving and receiving (4:8–5:1).
- Love means risking the possibility of pain (5:2–6:3).
- Words fail for expressing love (6:4–7:9).
- Love must be given freely (7:10–13).
- True love is priceless (8:1–14).

God is the source of all kinds of love, and He places love in the human heart for us to relate to each other as the Godhead relates to each other. The believer must then actualize that love. God is love and the man or woman who receives God, receives love. God commanded husbands to love their wives. He gave birth to unconditional love when He redeemed man.

Paul's command to Christians to love speaks of the nature of love as self-giving as seen in Galatians 5:13–15. The Christian walk is to be characterized by love as Paul speaks of, "walking in love," in Romans 14:15. The Christian should increase and abound in love. (See 1 Thessalonians 3:12.)

Love is vitally connected with faith in that the believer's faithful response is one of love. Love is also connected with hope. Christian love is evidence of God's purpose for His children. The Johannine writings magnify the significance of love as forcefully and fully as any other writings. John's writings account for only one-tenth of the New Testament, but they provide one-third of the references to love. The key passage is Jesus' new commandment in John 13:34–35, "A new command I give you: Love one another. As I have loved you, so you must love one another. By this all men will know that you are my disciples, if you love one another."

Jesus' command, that we love one another, gives us insight into the nature of His desire for the church—the nature of Christian love. What is commanded is not an emotion. It is the disciplined will to seek the welfare of others. Jesus speaks with the authority of the Father, the only One with authority to make such demands of men and women. Jesus speaks as the incarnate Word. (See John 1:1, 14.) He has authority to give conditions for discipleship. Notice the relationship of this commandment to that found in Leviticus 19:18. Both passages command love, but Jesus' commandment includes the clause, "As I have loved you."

The letters of John make explicit statements about the ethical implications of love. Our appreciation of these letters and the command to love is increased when we realize John's opponents claimed they loved God despite their unlovely temper and conduct. They claimed enlightenment and communion with God. (They were Gnostics or "Knowers.") The Old Testament, which was John's basis for Christians, portrays belief in Jesus and love for one another. (See 1 John 3:23.) This love is to be manifested in deeds. (See 1 John 3:18.) John left no doubt about the relationship of love and belief in God. Whoever hates his brother is in darkness. (See 1 John 2:9.) Whoever does not do right and love his brother is not of God. (See 1 John 4:20.) First John 4:8 is the climax, "He that loveth not knoweth not God; for God is love" (KJV).

The simple theme of 1 Corinthians 13 reveals the power of love. An outline of that chapter declares the importance of love (vv. 1–3); the acts of love (vv. 4–7); the permanence of love (vv. 8–12); and the supremacy of love (v. 13).

All through the Old and New Testaments we see how important love is for the community of faith and marriage. Therefore, if love is the main hallmark of Christianity, how much more, then, should this love be practiced by redeemed husbands and wives?

Many of our Christian husbands and wives have entered into their relationships with faulty scriptural interpretations on submission, headship, the glory of the woman and silence in the church. As a result, their relationships are not full of love as the heavenly Father designed them to be. Faulty interpretation of Scripture causes many marriages to go sour, and ultimately, they end with abuse. But there is hope!

It is a difficult task to truly love someone we do not fully know or understand. To know in this sense refers to an acquired knowledge of the male or female specie according to the design of the Creator. One of the major reasons many couples are failing in their love relationships is based on faulty experiences (culture and tradition), lack of understanding each other, and lack of knowledge about how to express their love to each other.

It appears to be difficult for some men to fully understand women emotionally. But men can know about women from a theological point of view and ultimately can appreciate and love them as the Word commands.

Likewise, women can know and understand their husbands if they will commit to study the ways of their spouses and apply the appropriate approach that allows a flood of love to flow in the marriage.

Some of the biggest hindrances to great love relationships in marriages are theological, psychological, and emotional love busters.

Dr. Willard J. Harley Jr. discusses five different types of emotional love busters in his book, *The Love Busters*, which have been outlined[3]:

1. *Angry outbursts.* Deliberate attempts by your spouse to hurt you because of anger toward you. They are usually in the form of verbal or physical attacks.

2. *Disrespectful judgments.* Attempts by your spouse to change your attitudes, beliefs, and behavior by trying to force you into his/her way of thinking. If (1) he/she lectures you instead of respectfully discusses issues, (2) feels that his/her opinion is superior to yours, (3) he/she talks over you or prevents you from having a chance to explain your position, or (4) he/she ridicules your point of view, engaging in disrespectful judgments.

3. *Annoying behavior.* The two basic types of annoying behavior are habits and activities. Habits are repeated without much thought, such as the way your spouse eats or sits in a chair. Activities are usually scheduled and require thought to complete, such as attending sporting events or a personal exercise program. Habits and activities are "annoying behavior" if they cause you to feel unhappy. They can be as innocent as snoring or as destructive as infidelity or alcohol addiction.

4. *Selfish demands.* Attempts by your spouse to force you to do something for him/her, usually with implied threat of punishment if you refuse.

5. *Dishonesty.* Failure of your spouse to reveal his/her thoughts, feelings, habits, likes, dislikes, personal history, daily activities, and plans for the future. Dishonesty is not only providing false information about any of the above topics, but it is also leaving you with what he/she knows is a false impression.[4]

   Dr. Harley defines love busters as "habits that drain the love bank." I will not discuss the love busters, because I think his book is a must-read for every couple and a keeper for their library. However, following chapter 4, I will discuss some of the theological love busters that have been crippling Christian marriages over the centuries, which minimize the love factor in marriage. If couples would function by the proper biblical model for a loving relationship, we would not have the divorce epidemic we have in the western churches today.

## DISCUSSION

1. How do you build your friendships?

2. Do you do things (recreational/social) together?

3. Do you share moments together?

4. Do you take vacations alone with your spouse—without the children?

5. What are your thoughts on the types of love mentioned?

6. How do they relate to your marriage?

7. Do you find it difficult to give or accept unconditional love?

8. Do you nourish and cherish your spouse?

9. If you nourished and cherished your spouse, would there be a change in your relationship?

*Chapter 3*

## ECSTASY RESTORED

*Many waters cannot quench love; rivers cannot wash it
away. If one were to give all the wealth of his house for love,
it would be utterly scorned.*

—SONG OF SOLOMON 8:7

GOD'S DIVINE ORDER of creation was designed so that His
masterpiece—man—was created last. He created everything
for man's fulfillment, enjoyment, and employment, and planted a
garden eastward in Eden, then gave it to Adam as his new home.
The garden was luscious, fruitful, and rich with all the necessary
splendor of an oriental garden. Eden signifies delight and pleasure.
It was adorned with every tree pleasant to the sight and enriched
with every tree that yielded tasty fruit that was good for food.
God, as a tender Father, created a place of pleasure and fulfillment
for Adam and Eve. It was a paradise designed for two lovers.

The love relationship between Adam and Eve in the garden was
divine, sublime, and perfect. It is important to note, God placed
Adam in the garden before Eve was created. (See Genesis 2:15.)
Adam was a loving nurturer and gardener of Eden for the Garden of Eden. The psalmist may have reflected on the nurturing
spirit that was placed in man, through Adam, which led him to
say, "Blessed are all who fear the Lord....Your wife will be like a
fruitful vine within your house; your sons will be like olive shoots
around your table" (Ps. 128:1, 3).

Here is another important part of the creation puzzle. The animals were created according to their kinds, and "God blessed them
and said, 'Be fruitful and increase in number and fill the water
in the seas, and let the birds increase on the earth'" (Gen. 1:22,
NIV). But Adam was unable to be a progenitor of his kind. After
Adam started the ministry assigned to him and God saw how well
he handled himself, God was pleased with Adam's stewardship

and loyalty to the task. To complement Adam and assist him in this new pursuit, God decided to make him a helpmate, another human being as a suitable companion. (See Genesis 2:18.)

According to the Genesis account, God put Adam to sleep, took a rib from his side, and formed a woman to be his companion and colaborer. He did not take a bone from Adam's head to create a two-headed monster, nor did He take a bone from his feet to make her inferior or a slave. Instead, God took a rib from Adam's side so the woman could work alongside him and share equally in the blissful experience of marriage.

In their book titled *Premarital and Remarital Counseling*, Dr. Robert Stahmann and William J. Hiebert contend:

> The Second Chapter of the Book of Genesis addresses the nature of the man-woman relationship: "It is not good that man should be alone; I will make him a helper fit for him," (v. 18). Many have interpreted the word *helper* to mean *helpmate*; however, it would be better-translated, "Another human being, like or corresponding to him." The original Hebrew says, "another person [woman] to live alongside him."[1]

Various scholars have different interpretations for the word *helper* in verse 18 which just muddy the plain scriptural truth. The scripture is clear about this fact, there is no ambiguity. God made Adam a wife from his rib to work along with him in the garden and to be progenitors. He did not make another man for Adam, He made a female and this is the pattern God establishes as the norm for marriage.

The very moment God presented Eve as a companion to Adam, and his eyes beheld her, he was immediately drawn to her in love. She satisfied his loneliness and need for a companion. Thus, he gave her identity and security when he uttered, "This is now bone of my bones and flesh of my flesh" (Gen. 2:23). His words denoted a kinship and equality between the two. Adam regarded Eve as the completeness of his flesh and was saying, "We are one. I will love, nurture, and care for you as I have done successfully to all God has put under my care." He was also saying, "I will cultivate you with my love. I will bring out the beauty in you and sustain the glory of your womanhood, gifts, and femininity."

Adam, being the first person to see and experience life, was to lead his wife on the path he had trod and those paths he had not yet trod, but together they would continue in love and submission. It was not difficult for Eve to sit back and listen to Adam, her lover, as he rehearsed the names and characters of the various animals. Eve even noticed how well they listened and obeyed his words and motions. It was in love that she joined with him—working and serving together. It is important to note that despite the Fall and Adam's blame of Eve when he said to God, "The woman you put here with me—she gave me some fruit from the tree, and I ate it," Adam still remained faithful in his love for Eve (Gen. 3:12).

It was Thomas Bradbury, in his book *The Development Course of Marital Dysfunction,* who said:

> Adam was the figure of the Coming One—the Last Adam. The popular notion is that Eve beguiled Adam. Eve did nothing of the kind. Satan beguiled her by throwing the dust of fleshly expectancy in her eyes and allured her into transgression against God resulting in distancing herself from Him. The Holy Spirit tells us plainly 'Adam was not deceived, but the woman being deceived became a transgressor' (1 Tim. 2:14). Adam was in no way deceived, neither by the devil nor by his wife. He knew what he was doing and blatantly sinned. He saw Eve in the depths of her guilt and shame; and out of pure love for her, he chose to be damned with her. He cleaved to his wife, for they were one flesh; and into ruin he plunged himself for her sake. In all this he was the figure of Him that was to come, yet very much unlike Him. Adam loved the creature more than the Creator did. Christ loved the Father with the same love that He bore to His bride, the church.[2]

Thomas Bradbury's view seems very palatable—a reason for Adam's choice of action. However, we should note that Adam had experienced a wonderful love relationship with God when he met and communed with Him in the cool of the day. He experienced *agape* love, *storge* love, and *phileo* love. Adam enjoyed that time of fellowship, communing, and bonding with his Creator. Adam felt loved, he felt friendship, and he felt secure with God. It is also important to note Adam saw how the animals around him demonstrated love to their kind. Then God created a wife for Adam so he could demonstrate his love to her. It was Adam's responsibility to teach Eve about love since he had experienced it in his relationship with God. Love is obedience to the laws of God.

Adam's sin ruined his family and the entire human race. Sin brought death and dysfunction to the first family. Amidst the crisis in the first family, it was still Adam's responsibility as the head and leader of his family to continue the loving relationship with Eve. Sin does not excuse husbands from their responsibility to show love to their wives, and Adam proved that as he cared for Eve.

When Eve sinned, by eating from the "tree of the knowledge of good and evil," she disobeyed the law of God. (See Genesis 2:17.) Adam had a choice to redeem her in love, but instead he disobeyed God's command and died spiritually and physically with her. The sins of Adam and Eve marred their love relationship and their lives. God's love pattern was now altered. God made man to have a pure love toward Him and toward his mate. In love, God gave us the Second Adam—Jesus Christ. Jesus gave His life for His Bride, the church, and rescued her from the powers of sin and death. Through Jesus Christ, mankind is redeemed and lives are restored.

Amidst the crisis in the first family, Adam and Eve stayed together in love and weathered the storms of separation from the Garden of Eden and the murder of their son Abel by his brother Cain. Love is not easy. Love can cause pain, bitterness, resentment, and disappointment; but, if you keep giving love, it will hide a multitude of faults, sins, errors, or flaws, and will ultimately replace all negatives with positives. If it is love that brings two lives and hearts together as one, and if God is an essential part of that equation, then whatever circumstances may come their way, a married couple can salvage their love relationship just as the first family, Adam and Eve, did.

The Garden of Eden suffered a great physical loss when sin

entered. Adam and Eve were cast out of the garden to live in a place that was not as pleasant as Eden had been, but they kept the garden within their hearts as they shared love and enjoyed life to the fullest. They lived together weathering various family problems, and they died at an old age still loving each other. (See Genesis 5:5.)

Problems will always be a part of marriage. However, when love is present there will be healing and resolution. If you have love, regardless of the present circumstances, you can repair the broken pieces of your love relationship.

How can you cultivate love or use love to heal the hurt individuals experience in marriage? The following chapter will discuss the types of love and how to use them to maximize and build your relationship.

## DISCUSSION

1. What type of love did Adam have that kept him and Eve together through life-changing experiences?

2. Is that love available today?

3. Do we have to run away from our homes and our family responsibilities because of the sins within the families?

4. Do you agree with Thomas Bradbury's view on Adam?

5. Discuss the reasons why you agree or disagree.

*Chapter 4*

# THE LOVING THING TO DO

*My lover is mine and I am his.*
            —SONG OF SOLOMON 2:16, NIV

MORE AND MORE homes are disintegrating. Families are dysfunctional. Children are being reared in one-parent families and often abused. Families need to turn to God for guidance, and husbands must follow the command to love their wives as stated in Ephesians 5:25. Older women need to follow the biblical call to teach younger wives how to love their husbands.

The command to love one's wife as Christ loves the church is a mammoth task for husbands. Jesus' love for the church led Him to the cross. His love was one of sacrifice. His love for the church is the model for man's love for his wife. But, is it possible to achieve this model? Did God command man to do the impossible? On the contrary! Achieving this goal is possible! Christ has made it possible for man to love his wife unconditionally if he receives the enabler—the Holy Spirit.

Before Paul commanded husbands to love their wives in Ephesians 5:25, he commanded wives to submit to their own husbands (v. 22). Before Paul commanded the brothers and sisters to submit to each other in the Lord (v. 21), he commanded them to be "filled with the Spirit" (v. 8).

God gave men the Holy Spirit to help them achieve the greatest ideal for marriage. Without the aid of the Holy Spirit, it is impossible for husbands to love their wives as Christ outlined in His Word and wives to voluntarily submit to her husband's loving headship.

                    31

## Husbands "Gift" to Love

God designed and created the perfect gift for man—woman. He made woman by using the rib of Adam as His raw material; she was created to complement and complete Adam. She was presented to Adam as a perfect and permanent gift; one who would be a lifetime partner to love and cherish, and one who would fill all his needs for companionship, pleasure, and procreation. She was designed as a suitable partner. No other animal could replace her, and neither was there any other created being that could take her place in the life of Adam.

When God presented Adam with this "gift," his wife, Adam confessed she was indeed a suitable and compatible partner for him when he said, "Bone of my bones and flesh of my flesh…" (Gen. 2:23).

Before Adam received his gift he lived a less-than-complete life. He was lonely. He had no one with whom to share his thoughts and no one to share his dreams. He had no one to work alongside him; however, when he was given Eve, his life was finally complete and his world was changed.

I believe husbands of today still need to see their wives as gift given by God to be loved and cherished. There are many husbands who see their wives as gifts on the day they are married. After the wedding and the honeymoon is over, they no longer see them as gifts of God, but as possessions they own and control. Wives are not the property of men. Instead, they are gifts from God and as such, husbands must honor God's gift by loving their wives as Christ loves the church.

Scripture teaches that a marriage based and founded on love is a complete, fulfilled, and successful marriage. Husbands are lifted up in Scripture as the head of their families. Scripture calls husbands to lead their families, by loving their wives—their gifts from God.

In order to love their wives in the manner required, husbands must understand not only the original design of wives as gifts, but also the evolutionary process women have gone through. Methods and ways of demonstrating love have changed every decade. It is the responsibility of each husband to discover ways of showing love to his wife and keeping that love alive.

In a CNN report which was aired in October 1997, a revealing statistic showed that while only 15 percent of wives worked outside the home in 1955, by 1990, that percentage had increased to 55 percent.[1] These changes in the role of women have influenced how husbands show love to their wives. Because many husbands today are no longer the sole financial provider of the household, they must learn to deal with that situation. When they come home from work, their wives will also be coming home from work. They will both be tired. Therefore, both must learn to communicate and agree on ways they can demonstrate love toward each other.

In order for husbands to truly love their wives, they need to understand the love relationship between Jesus and the church and the standard He set—how men and women were made and how women were treated in Bible times.

Christ loves the church by choice—voluntarily and freely—and has made it the object of His love. The church was, by nature, sinful. We know the church of Christ is made up of people who are actually defiled by their own transgressions; but the kind of love Jesus bestows on the church is that of a husband. His love is special, constant, true, and intense. It is saturated with appreciation for the original design, evolutionary process, and potential for the church. It is not mere lip service. By nature the church is not yet perfected for Christ, but by grace He entitled her to His love and forgiveness. It is important to note that neither wives nor husbands are perfect. However, it is the husband's responsibility to give love to his wife as a gift of grace, so that together they will become whole in the marriage union.

In the garden, Adam and Eve were created equal and complemented each other. (See Genesis 1:27–28; 2:18–23.) The New Testament teaches that in Christ this edenic completeness is restored. (See 2 Corinthians 5:17; Galatians 3:28; and Ephesians 5:21–33.) Mates are equal (see 1 Corinthians 7:4) and interdependent (see 1 Corinthians 11:11–12.) The new creation in Christ makes that possible.

The fall, however, ruptured God's plan for male/female equality and produced sin. Sin produced male dominance and female submissiveness. (See Genesis 3:16.) Hence, many scholars believe male dominance and female submissiveness are "descriptive rather than prescriptive."

Careful investigation of the Old Testament, specifically the Book of Genesis, reveals that much of Scripture describes a double standard for male superiority and female inferiority; a kind of "chain of command," where the husband is found ruling his wife and children. Different standards of fidelity in marriage are also quite apparent in Old Testament Scripture.

Unfaithful wives were dealt with more severely than were husbands. (See Numbers 5:11–31; Deuteronomy 22:22–29.) However, the New Testament's response was that of mutual equality and servanthood toward each other with the servanthood of Jesus as the basic criterion. (See Ephesians 5:21–33.)

In the eyes of Christ, husbands and wives are equal. However, in light of functions, the Bible teaches an order for marriage. The order is simple—it is the husband as the loving head who should be giving loving care to his wife; and the wife should voluntarily submit to the loving care of her husband. When this method is adhered to, even the children will follow suite in the family hierarchical structure as outlined in Ephesians 6:1–3:

> Children, obey your parents in the Lord, for this is right. Honor your father and mother—which is the first commandment with a promise—that it may go well with you and that you may enjoy long life on the earth.

Wives are not only given as gifts to their husbands, but also as gifts to work alongside of their husbands as they serve their families, churches, communities, nations, and the world. Throughout the New Testament, we find examples of husbands and wives teaming actively and involved in ministry. Today, the same examples can be found in many marriages. However, there are many husbands who do not love their wives as equals and helpmates.

While traveling home on a flight from Tortola, the Virgin Islands, I read an interesting article in *American Way* magazine titled, "I Know What Love Is," by Jim Shahin.[2]

Mr. Shahin said while he was driving his car, and listening to

Prince's rousing song to immortal love, "I Would Die 4 U," he found out what Prince's idea of love was. "You!" Prince shouted. "I would die for you."

Singing along with Prince, Jim was not the least bit concerned that the woman in the car next to him was wary of him. As she locked her door and reached for her cell phone, Jim convulsed and banged on the steering wheel of his car as he sang along with Prince. The song questioned, "What if it seemed to her I was a lunatic?" Then it continued: "I am a lunatic. I am a lunatic of love. I would die for you, darling, if you want me to."

While he sang, Jim suddenly understood the meaning of the song, and he said, "No, you would not, Prince. You would not die for anybody. You are just saying that because it sounds good."

Jim said that in reality Prince would not die for anybody he loved, and few other people would do it either. It was a song with hollow words.

People say they will climb mountains, swim oceans, and even die, all to prove their love. But the reality is they will probably never have to prove it. Wives are not interested in their husbands dying for them. Most women only ask that their husbands express their love in small ways.

Suppose a husband said to his wife, "Honey, I have decided I am going to prove my love for you, so I am leaving today and will be gone for six months to climb Mount Everest. Kiss the kids for me. Do not forget to pay the gas bill. I love you. Bye." What does that kind of love prove? It certainly does not prove the couple had a marriage that God wants for His families.

Love does not focus on self; it is giving, serving, and sharing. By climbing the mountain, the man would be expressing love—not for his wife, but for his sport. He loved the sport of mountain climbing more than he loved his wife and their children.

Jesus gave Himself for the church—His bride. (See Ephesians 5:25.) He is the supreme model of unconditional love, and it should be noted that Jesus' directive was not for husbands to die for their wives, but to love their wives. (See v. 28.) Nevertheless, if the ultimate test of death presents itself, the husband should be ready to pay the price.

The command for husbands to love their wives is both simple and complex. The easiest way to show love is in the mundane things. It is giving her a foot massage or making a sandwich and giving her the bigger portion. Show your wife love by telling her you like her new hairstyle, by picking up after yourself, loading and unloading the dishwasher, and by doing the small things that communicate the message of love and care.

True love is warming up the car in the wintertime before your wife leaves for work. It is going grocery shopping without complaining, then helping her prepare dinner. It is accepting your wife for who she is and, at the same time, helping her to be all she can be. It is expressing interest in her life—asking about her day. The greatest love can be shown through the little things you do for you wife. Give it some thought! The list is inexhaustible!

As each individual examines the nature of love and the makeup of the person he or she loves, the complexities of love are revealed. According to Harville Hendrix, PhD, in his book, *Keeping the Love You Find,* "Real love is an achievement of consciousness and intentionality, a way of being, a hard-won prize granted only to those who persevere."[3]

The command God gave to husbands to love their wives was not an afterthought. Paul gave the example of showing love by using Christ's love for the church as the model. (See Ephesians 5:23.) Paul was motivated to give this command because he wanted to correct the Greek, Roman, and Jewish cultural viewpoints on women in general, and wives in particular. A careful reading of the Bible reveals that women were never *commanded* to love their husbands. Instead, they were *encouraged* to love their husbands. Paul admonishes the older women to "teach the young women to be sober, to love their husbands, to love their children" (Titus 2:4, KJV).

Cynthia Heald states in her book, *Loving Your Husband*, that in Titus 2:4, "The Greek word *philandros* is used to express 'loving your husband.' It is from the root word *phileo*, which means to show affection, love, devotion, and hospitality. It speaks of being fond of friends and relatives."[4]

The account of the curse placed on women in Genesis 3:16

tells us that God said to the woman [Eve], "I will greatly multiply thy sorrow and thy conception; in sorrow thou shalt bring forth children; and thy desire shall be to thy husband," (KJV). We could conclude from the phrase "thy desire," that the curse produced the inclination and longing in the heart of Eve toward Adam, and subsequently, all women toward the men in their lives.

Science now explains to us what happens when a man and woman participate in sexual intercourse. Oxytocin produces a bond between the couple. However, the effect of the bond or inclination is greater from the woman to the man than the man to the woman.

Nevertheless, by the nature of the curse, a "longing after" was motivated by an intrinsic love for her husband; thus, becoming natural for all other women through the gene of federal mother, Eve. The Hebrew word *teshuwaqah*, interpreted as "desire," means, "sense of stretching out after"—a longing. Eve submitted to Adam in love as her natural demeanor before and after the Fall. She remained with him, gave birth to children, and lived with him until death. They were joined together in love. They lived together in love. She did not allow sin, sickness, or murder to separate her from her husband and family.

By nature, women were created to function at their best in a loving, nurturing environment. Once women get connected to the source of love, they will submit to the loving care in partnership.

Women are love seekers. They are attached or magnetized to love. When they are given love by their husbands, they will seek to submit to the loving care and work to fulfill God's will for their lives and the marriage union.

The Creation story declared that Adam and Eve were created equally in the image of God, and that they were given rule over everything. They ruled together. The sinful Fall in the Garden of Eden brought woman under the rule of the man. However, Christ Jesus died and redeemed man and woman and brought them back into their original state when He became the Second Adam. Once a man and woman accept the finished work of Calvary, they are restored to the perfect image of God. Therefore, husbands should love their wives as copartners and helpmates.

Within our church circle we are inundated with calls in sermons, sermonettes, and comments for wives to be submissive to their husbands; yet, little emphasis is placed upon husbands loving their wives. A careful reading of the Bible reveals that more emphasis is placed on a husband's role to his wife than on the wife's role to her husband. Therefore, as preachers proclaim and teach the gospel, they should carefully prepare, and then present, a balanced message about marriage when sharing God's Word. Ministers must be thorough and comprehensive in the task.

A typical instance is found in Ephesians 5:22–24 when Paul said, "Wives, submit to your own husband as to the Lord. For the husband is the head of the wife, as also Christ is the head of the church; and He is the Savior of the body. Therefore just as the church is subject to Christ, so let the wives be to their own husbands in everything" (NKJV). That directive took only three verses, but reference to the husband's role in marriage took nine verses:

> Husbands, love your wives, just as Christ also loved the church, and gave Himself for her, that He might sanctify and cleanse her with the washing of water by the word, that He might present her to Himself a glorious church, not having spot, or wrinkle or any such thing; but that she should be holy and without blemish. So husbands ought to love their own wives as their own bodies; he who loves his wife loves himself. For no one ever hated his own flesh, but nourishes and cherishes it, just as the Lord does the church: For we are members of His body, of His flesh, and of His bones. For this reason a man shall leave his father and mother, and be joined to his wife, and the two shall be one flesh. This is a great mystery: but I speak concerning Christ and the church. Nevertheless, let each one of you in particular so love his own wife as himself, and let the wife see that she respects her husband.
>
> —EPHESIANS 5:25–33, NKJV

The crisis in the text is magnified by the extended discourse addressing the problem, the word picture, and the illustration cited.

We are living in a time when it seems dysfunctional homes,

divorced parents, and single-parent families are the norm, and functional families are abnormal. Statistics report an alarming growth in single parenting and a decline in two-parent families.

In 1998, the United States Census Bureau reported that 38 percent of Americans were single adults. In a November 4, 1998 broadcast, the American Broadcasting Corporation's (ABC) news-magazine *20/20* reported 53 percent of African American and 18 percent of Caucasian mothers were single parents. It was predicted, given the sociological trends, that single adults would be 50 percent of the American adult population by the year 2000.[5]

Even in our churches today we find many men separating from their wives and children for various reasons. Abuse is rampant in both single-parent and two-parent families, in Christian and non-Christian families. Many homes do not offer a sense of security to the female members. Sometimes females become prey to their own brothers, fathers, or stepfathers, and other male members of their families. It is even more alarming that some of those men claim to be Christians.

Let me share with you some simple and practical ideas to consider.

Love is not always complex. It is usually the little things in life that add spice and beauty to love. A major reason for the many dysfunctional homes among North American families is the lack of love between husbands and wives—specifically the husband's love for his wife. Thanks be to God that men are beginning to reclaim their divinely ordained position in God. An example of this is the Million-Man March on October 16, 1995 in which Louis Farrakhan (one of the Muslin leaders in North America) challenged black men to reclaim their rightful place in their homes, communities, and churches. One problem with the march, however, was it failed to emphasize that men cannot claim their rightful place in society until they reconcile with Jesus Christ. That has to be achieved first.

There was another million-man march on October 4, 1997 in Washington DC by the Promise Keepers, when men of all races, status, and social classes came together, confessed their sins, and pledged to reclaim their rightful places in God's design for men in their families. Their good intentions were criticized, though. The National Organization for Women (NOW) was outraged, claiming the movement was another white-collar men's movement trying to enslave their wives again and to put them under bondage. The opposite, of course, was true. There have been many reports and testimonies from wives all over North America of how their husbands came home renewed and rejuvenated, as well as more loving and compassionate toward them and their children.

A husband (name withheld for privacy) who went to his first Promises Keepers conference in June 1997, at RFK Stadium, in Washington DC said, "That very 'wet' weekend has helped to change my life around. I asked my wife of over twenty-three years to marry me all over again on Sunday, February 14, 1999, and she did."

Another man by the name of Billy, (this is not his real name) said:

> Eight years ago, I went through a terrible divorce. I made many awful mistakes and I left two kids behind. Since my divorce, I have married a wonderful woman with three kids. Two years ago, all was not well and the stepfather thing was not working. During that year, I attended the Memphis PK conference. Believe it or not, my boss sort of manipulated me to go.
>
> As soon as I walked into the stadium and heard approximately 50,000 men singing praises to the Lord, I was broken. The main thing I remember is that I cried for the entire weekend. I cried over leaving my two kids in my first marriage, I cried over the tough time I was having with my step kids, and I cried because I knew I was not much of a husband, a father, or a man—what a mess!
>
> When I got home from Memphis, I was determined to be a dad to all of my kids. I wanted to be responsible. The two years since my first PK conference have been awesome. All of my children, all five of them, are doing well. I have a relationship with each one of them. God has given me a family, and I love them very much. I have really made an effort to be responsible to those I love. It feels so good to do the right thing.

This year, in Little Rock, my 16-year-old stepson and I attended a PK conference together. It was so great to stand and praise God together! My relationship with my stepson is nothing short of a God-given miracle. I still have a lot to learn, but I just wanted to say thanks for showing me how to leave a legacy. Trust me, I thank God daily for what I have now.

Most men went home from that Promise Keepers meeting with their consciences raised and with a deeper commitment to family values. However, even if the experiences received by the men at the Promise Keepers meeting were short lived, it was worth the little changes that took place in homes. I have read the confessions and testimonies of many men who attended those meetings, and I can say with certainty, Promise Keepers does not need to apologize for positive outcomes.

Another men's group was recently formed called The Men of the Titanic. The group was organized to honor the bravery and valor of men who had given their lives in watery graves for their wives. A few women, who wanted to keep the memory of those men alive, started The Men of the Titanic. Their theme was We Will Not Forget. The ladies eventually faded out, but later a group of men resurrected the movement to honor the memories, lives, and love stories of the men of the Titanic. They pledged to adopt the same philosophy the original organization had in their relationships with their wives. The simple philosophy of the movement is each man pledges to love his wife until the point of death. Those men declare, if a decision is made that would take the life of their wives, they will volunteer their lives instead so their wives can be saved—as many of the men did in the real Titanic tragedy. It is encouraging that this mens group is motivated by such high morals and standards, and its motivation was reignited with the debut of the movie *Titanic*.

We men are no longer our own, but sons of God through the reconciliation of Jesus Christ. We are motivated to love our wives whom God has given us, even to the point of death if the ultimate test should come.

When the command for husbands to love their wives was

given, it did not mean to subjugate, exert power, manipulate, coerce, intimidate, or abuse. The command means husbands should serve their wives. It begins first with the husbands biblically loving their wives.

Husbands are commanded to love their wives with God's love. That is, God's unconditional love. Love is neither a seasonal nor a one-time event. It is an ongoing, unconditional exercise. Some men may need to revive that love. Whatever they need to do, God is holding husbands responsible for their families by how well they love their wives.

A recent statistic revealed one of every three church leaders' wives is abused. *Silent Suffering...Silent Shame*, a video produced by the Church of God Womens Ministries Department in Cleveland, Tennessee, suggests women are abused in the following ways:

Emotionally—They experience lack of self-worth.
Physically—They are beaten and misused.
Verbally—They are spoken to condescendingly.[6]

The statistic reveals that one-third of church leaders' wives are not getting the love that is mandated by God. If that is true, what is the percentage among the laity? In many cases, much of the laity has comparatively limited knowledge of God's Word. Husbands in church roles should be models for the husbands among the laity.

It is disturbing, but some fathers show more love to their children than they do to their wives. Men are to love their children, but the love for their wives should not conflict with that love. Giving romance, money, and gifts does not fulfill God's call for husbands to love their wives. Those things are superficial, even though they are signs of love to some women. Even if you give your wife all the tangible items she desires, she still may be missing genuine love. Many husbands are good men, good fathers, and good providers, but they are poor lovers. Many husbands only give love to their wives at special times. The command to love your wife is not seasonal. It is a command for all times.

Love is the only thing a husband can give his wife to make her completely happy and satisfied. All other things are secondary and not fully satisfying, but when they get love, they have it all. Love is the ultimate, love is infinite, and most of all, love is priceless.

It is amazing to look at some couples. As they grow older they become more close-knit in their love relationship. On the other hand, there are some couples who drift apart the longer they live together. Love should create a bond that, with time, is unbreakable. If a man does not find his wife more attractive, more appealing, and more appetizing as time passes, then he needs to check his "love thermometer" to see what is wrong. That refers not only to physical beauty but also to inner beauty, character, and grace.

Husbands, your wives are beautiful; they are as precious jewels. Your love and attention will keep them shining, glowing, glittering, and blooming. Loving does not necessarily mean physical love, but holistic love. It is a shame that in some couples' bedrooms—the place where the highest form of physical love should be demonstrated between a loving couple—the experience leaves much to be desired.

God designed women to function best in an environment of love. If true love is given, a wife will be able to function in the service God has set for her.

As I close this portion of the chapter, I would like to share with you Dr. Harley's top five ways wives like their husbands to express love to them as outlined in his book *His Need, Her Needs.*[7]

*Affection*—According to Dr. Harley, this is the number one emotional need of wives. Wives want to hear from their husbands how much they love and care for them. To help husbands who have difficulty expressing affection, Dr. Harley makes the following suggestions:

- Hug and kiss your wife. Tell her you love her every morning while you are still in bed. Rub her back for a few minutes before you get up.

- Tell her you love her while you are having breakfast together.

- Kiss her and tell her you love her before you leave for work.

- Call her during the day, ask how she is doing. Tell her you love her.

- After work, call her before you leave to tell her when you will be home. Tell her you love her.

- Buy her flowers on the way home at least once a week, with a card that tells her you love her.

- When you arrive home from work, give her a big hug and kiss and spend a few minutes talking to her about how her day went. Do not do anything else before you have given her your undivided attention.

- Tell her you love her as you are having dinner together.

- Help her clear off the table. Wash and dry the dishes with her. Give her a hug and kiss at least once, then tell her you love her.

- Hug and kiss her. Tell her you love her in bed before you both go to sleep.

—ADAPTED FROM WWW.MARRIAGEBUILDERS.COM

*Conversation*—Set apart time each day to just talk with your wife. The need for conversation is not met by simply talking to someone. It is met when the conversation is enjoyable for both. Good conversation is characterized by the following: (1) Using it to inform and investigate each other; (2) focusing attention on topics of mutual interest; (3) balancing the conversation so both have an equal opportunity to talk; and (4) giving each other undivided attention while talking to each other. Conversation provides the opportunity for intimate sharing and bonding time for women, and husbands need to learn how to communicate with their wives to meet this emotional need. God made women to be more verbal, whereas, husbands seem to become verbally challenged after marriage. If conversation was an integral part of your courtship experience, you can reignite it by following the above guideline to liven up your marriage.

*Honesty and openness*—Honesty and openness must first begin with God before people can be fully open in the mutual context of a beneficial relationship. Honesty and openness provide a sense of security and bonding. When wives get accurate information about their spouses' thoughts, feelings, habits, likes, dislikes, personal history, daily activities, and plans for the future it helps to build their trust and love. When spouses openly reveal the facts of their past, their present activities, and plans for the future they are better able to make intelligent decisions that take feelings into account and make the marriage bond strengthen.

*Financial support*—Financial support provides financial security for wives. Many wives might not have married their husbands for money, but they expect to have money to meet their every need and more. They expect to know there is some form of arrangement made should death come, that they will have a financially secure future. In a nutshell, your wife wants to know you assume responsibility to feed, clothe, and shelter the family.

*Family contentment*—Wives feel loved and appreciated when their husbands become active in the moral and educational development of the children. Children are products of both parents and when husbands take responsibility for how the children turn out by teaching them the values of cooperation and care for each other, they are depositing a lot of love. Spending quality time with your children helps ensure happiness and success for them as adults. When you, as the loving husband, participate in family activities it guarantees a better life for your children and the outcome will deposit so much love that it will trigger her feeling of love for you.

## WIVES—LOVING THEIR HUSBANDS

> That they may teach the young women to be sober, to love their husbands, to love their children.
> —TITUS 2:4, KJV

Do wives really need to know how to love their husbands? If they did not need to know, the Holy Spirit would not have instructed Paul to direct Titus on the method how to do so. The

Bible does not command women to love their husbands. As science reveals, once a wife experiences physical intimacy with her husband through sexual intercourse her body releases oxytocin, the bonding hormone, which creates a bond between she and her husband. The more they share love together, the more bonded and attached to each other they become. Oxytocin would probably explain why Scripture tells us wives will have a desire for their husbands. (See Genesis 3:16.)

If that is the case, as science explains, why should young wives be taught how to love their husbands? Well, when God instructed older women to teach younger women how to love their husbands in Titus 2:4, He used the word *phileo*. It means friendship love, a love that cherishes, enjoys, and likes—that was the intended message! Older women were encouraged to teach the younger wives the art and science of loving their husbands. That admonition was given to minimize the trial and error method many wives had to go through to maximize their marital relationships.

The writer encouraged Titus to employ the method because he was aware that women view love differently than men. Seeing that older wives had learned how to love their husbands through their years in marriage Paul instructed young Titus to have the older women teach the younger women. Paul did not instruct Titus to teach the younger women. Paul wanted the older women to teach because they were better able to address the issues from both experience and knowledge.

How can a wife nurture a heart of love, to support her husband in practical ways and build friendship to last "until death do us part"? Wives show love to their husbands first by fulfilling God's purpose and place in their marriage. They show love when they glorify God by illustrating the love relationship between Jesus Christ and His church. (See Ephesians 5:22–33.) She loves her husband by voluntarily submitting to his love and care. Secondly, she will respond to her husband's love needs out of godly purpose to fulfill and satisfy her husband.

Building a loving and lasting relationship takes daily commitment, prayer, and most of all, a decision to love your husband—no matter what. Using Christ's loving relationship with the church as your example, you can change your heart and become the wife God wants you to be. However, do not try loving your husband by using just your own abilities. Your husband may, at times, do something that disturbs or destroys your love and trust. Allow the Holy Spirit to love your husband through you. When you are able to love your husband through the Holy Spirit, you will be able to love him unconditionally.

Wives show love to their husbands by doing things that will build bonds of friendship. Therefore, commit yourself today to make your husband your number one human relationship. And, dare I say, that includes your children. Your relationship with your husband is meant to be the most important relationship, other than God's.

However, the truth of the matter is, many husbands' love needs suffer because some wives *over*-invest in their children and *under*-invest in their husbands. To prevent the dilemma, Paul called for the older wives to teach younger wives how to balance their love priority. Women are wired to be both mother and wife, and one should not suffer for the other. However, wise women will keep in their memory that they begin and end as a wife.

Now, let us delve a little deeper into the course of loving your husbands, to check and see if you love your husbands as you should. I would like to suggest you begin with a simple question, "Am I spoiling my husband rotten?" This is what loving your husband is really all about, spoiling him rotten as he does the same for you! If your answer to that question is yes, then, what you will be reading from here on for the rest of the chapter will be just revision for you. However, if your answer is not fully yes, this portion will help you learn how to really love your husband in a way he will appreciate.

If your husband is not a believer, Peter tells us in his epistle the life you lead is an evangelistic tool for the conversion of your husband. (See 1 Peter 3:1.)

I know marriages in Christian homes are failing at an alarming rate, and your living situation with a non-believer might not be better. However, you do not have to let your marriage fail like many others have if you have love. If you choose to follow the biblical mandate, God's grace will supply the love you need to have a successful marriage and hard times will just be hard times to help your marriage grow.

Love means different things to people; it also means different things to the sexes. In the beginning of the chapter I discussed the things women need to feel loved. The question now is, in what ways should you show love to your husband with purpose?

Christian wives consider it essential to keep God's purpose in view at all times when considering the responsibility to love their husbands. They realize God has not called them to meaningless activity in their marriage, but to a divine order and purpose. Showing love to your husband is designed to satisfy his needs and desires, not your own.

Love-based needs and desires are generated by human emotions. And one of the goals in marriage is to fulfill your mate's needs—because that is what love does. If we are to fulfill those needs, you must understand what they are. The problem is some people do not know or understand the difference between needs and wants. A desire for a new gun, computer, sports car, boat, or diamond ring does not qualify as a need—it is a want. Air, water, food, sex, and shelter are needs. Now we should be on the same track.

Husbands have needs. Love fulfills needs.

According to Dr. Harley, in his book *His Needs, Her Needs,* "emotional need: is a craving that, when satisfied, makes us feel happy and fulfilled, when unsatisfied, it makes us feel unhappy and frustrated."

As human beings we use emotional needs to measure how much love we are receiving. When those emotional needs are met it brings inner peace and satisfaction. Research was done to find out the top emotional needs of men to make a marriage satisfied. Dr. Harley Jr., gives us a list of the top five ways husbands appreciate love expressed by their wives.

## 1. Sexual fulfillment

God made your husband with a sex-drive need, and he has equipped you to be a perfect help suitable for that need. When husbands experience terrific sexual relationships with their wives, it fulfills their emotional and physical needs.

Husbands do not have control over that need by nature. That is the way God made man. The need is involuntary. Therefore, wives need to learn ways to satisfy that need in order to fulfill God's purpose and design for marriage.

One problem with that need is women do not usually have the same amount of sexual desire as men, and as a result they find it difficult to reach out to supply their husband needs. Hence, many wives suffer from "convenient" headaches, which is a cop-out. Convenient headaches, tiredness, pain, being sick, only to name a few, are those used to say, "I do not have that need now and you should not either." In which case, whose highest good is being sought?

How should you deal with your spouse's sexual needs? The apostle Paul gives the answer in 1 Corinthians 7:4–5, when he says, "The wife's body does not belong to her alone but also to her husband. In the same way, the husband's body does not belong to him alone but also to his wife. Do not deprive each other except by mutual consent and for a time, so that you may devote yourselves to prayer. Then come together again so that Satan will not tempt you because of your lack of self-control."

Christian wives, please take note that Satan always seems to know ones' weakest moments. He waited until Christ had been without food for forty days before he suggested bread for Him. Even so, Satan is aware, ready, and able to provide an unlawful fulfillment for those unmet sexual needs. If you really do love your husband and want to spoil him rotten, seek to fulfill his sexual needs to the best of your ability. Learn to cultivate a greater sexual appetite for your husband. Many sex experts tell us 90 percent of sex is in the mind. Begin by cultivating desires that will help you better supply your husband's and your sexual needs.

## 2. Recreational companionship

If your husband is your best friend, it is important that you share his interests in recreational activities. Many wives forget the things they did while they were dating. They did many things they would never have chosen to do alone, just to be with their date. God did not make another man for Adam for companionship. He created woman to be man's best friend. So, wives should never forget that. It is amazing when you take time to be with your husband; because of love, you will find yourself loving the things he loves and vice versa.

If possible, find things you both can enjoy as a starting point. As you build friendship you will realize it is not so much the activity that matters, it is the companionship. You will fulfill the highest good when you seek to show love in what satisfies your husband.

To be his friend is more important than a trip to the mall when he wants the mountains. Spending time together helps you make memories together and the more memories shared, the stronger the bond. Participating in your husband's recreational activities creates memories that, if you do not support them, may be shared with someone else. Spend time involving yourself with your husband's leisure activities. It will create pleasant memories for the two of you that can be cherished for years to come.

A mistake many young parents make is forgetting each other's need for companionship when their children come along. Do not allow children's wants and needs to take precedence over your husband's needs. While you do want your children to excel and be fulfilled, maybe even to fulfill some unmet need from your childhood, you risk leaving your husband alone with an unmet companionship need—that can create jealousy and problems within the marriage. If you involve your husband in the care of your children, it will provide you the opportunity to have the energy and time to see to his needs for companionship.

### 3. Physical attractiveness

Men are usually attracted to women by sight. Yes, there are other things that attract men to women, but physical attractiveness ranks high on the list. Therefore, satisfying your husband's need for love means you must keep yourself physically beautiful and fit, with a good diet and exercise. Take time to continue dressing up and making yourself attractive for your husband. Sometimes, wives complain their husbands do not look at them much, but if the truth be told, they do not give their husbands much to look at! Some wives feel that once they are married and have a ring, their appearance does not matter much anymore. Yes, it still matters.

Take time to keep yourself as the girl he married. Do not forget what attracted him to you. Time, children, and body changes will alter the physical look of the body, but you are gifted with the wisdom to maintain a satisfactory looking body if you choose.

If physical beauty is an important part of being an attractive wife to your husband, then do your best. An attractive spouse is more important to men than to women. Possibly, because men are visually stimulated.

## 4. Admiration

Men like to have their ego stroked and more so from their wives. Admiration and honor stroke their ego. Honor is due your husband, the head of the family, simply because he is the head—if for no other reason then that. However, if he is truly a loving husband, it should come naturally. Remember, God placed the responsibility for love and care for the family in the husband's hands, as some scholars say, because of seniority of creation and the deception of the woman. To the woman, He said, "Your desire shall be to your husband, and he shall rule over you" (Gen. 3:16).

Christian wives do accept Christ as the head of the church—as such, they honor and are subject to Him. Please realize, Paul is saying in that same way husbands are due the same honor.

When a Christian wife honors her husband, she shows him respect for who and what he is. She does not belittle, criticize, or complain about what her husband does or does not do, or of what she wants him to be. When you admire your husband for who he is, you will not want to make him over to suit your needs. Loving your husband means admiring and honoring him with all his ways, just as you married him. If you want change, give him love, and allow him to change by the love you give.

In 1 Peter chapter 3 the Amplified Bible Version gives a good description of how a wife should feel for her husband. "You are to feel for him all that reverence includes: to respect, defer to, revere him, to honor, esteem, appreciate, prize, and, in the human sense, to adore him, that is, to admire, praise, be devoted to, deeply love, and enjoy your husband" (v. 2). When a wife demonstrates those feelings of appreciation and honor toward her husband, she is laying groundwork for loving her husband rotten.

## 5. Domestic support

A husband's home is his castle, haven of rest. It is an environment that offers a refuge from stress and the rest of the world around him. Husbands feel loved when they come home to find a place of peace, tranquility, and quiescence. It makes no difference to the husband whether both work outside the home or not. When he enters his home, the man feels emotionally secure and at peace. But, if the home is filled with animosity, indifference, complaint, grip, and negative feelings, men have a tendency to turn to otherness to find peace. When you, as a wife, create an atmosphere that allows your husband to experience peace and wholeness, he will always look forward in coming home to the place where he knows his wife loves him rotten and wants to have him home to shower him with great love.

In conclusion, it is easy to love your husband or wife when he or she is loveable and kind. But you are to love unconditionally—no matter what. Love him or her even when it is hard, because that is when it will mean the most. Your love is a lifetime commitment made toward your spouse, not just when you feel like it or when you are in a good mood. *Love is not a feeling, it is an act of the will.* Make an extra effort to love your spouse at all times. Love will always win favor in your marriage.

When husbands sacrifice, nourish, cherish, honor, and understand their wives, they demonstrate "I love you" in caring for them. Wives should not view submission as an end; it is only a means to the end. Christian wives see the real target in God's sight as showering their husbands with a gentle rain of respect. It is the gift that best says to a man, "I love you." The beauty of marriage is that when love is expressed like that, it has a profound impact on each spouse. It actually sets in motion a circle of love that creates not only harmony, but also strength in marriage.

Ephesians 5:28–29 provides us with a good conclusion when it says, "Husbands ought also to love their own wives as their own bodies. He who loves his own wife loves himself; for no one ever hated his own flesh, but nourishes and cherishes it, just as Christ also does the church" (NASB). Ephesians 5:22, 33 says, "Wives, be subject to your own husbands, as to the Lord....The wife must see to it that she respects her husband" (NASB).

The text is saying, "Men feel loved when they are respected, and women feel loved when they are cared for." To fulfill those marriage needs, God gave husbands and wives two different lists of commands. Each one, if followed, will help meet the unique emotional needs of the opposite sex. Those needs can only be supplied through a servant who has a spirit-filled heart.

## DISCUSSION

1. Do you personally think it is possible to achieve the model of God's love for your marriage?

2. What are some of the things you think makes marriage so complex? So challenging?

3. Do you have to be reminded to love your wife/husband?

4. What are some ways you can express your love to your spouse?

5. What role does the Holy Spirit play in a marriage love relationship?

6. In what way was Eve a gift to Adam?

7. Why was she created?

8. What is the difference between a Scripture-based marriage and one that is not Scripture-based?

9. List and discuss some of the husband-and-wife teams in the New Testament.

10. Find out what your spouse's number one emotional need is.

11. Tell your spouse what you will to do fulfill that need.

## *Chapter 5*

## THE MISSING FACTOR

*And Adam said, "This is now bone of my bones, and flesh of my flesh: she shall be called Woman, because she was taken out of Man."*

—GENESIS 2:23, KJV

M ANY PEOPLE IN our culture underestimate the worth of women because the Scripture stories speak more of men. It is important to note the Bible was written by men, inspired of the Holy Spirit, to articulate the plan of God for His people—not to elevate one sex above the other. Both male and female play an active part in the evolutionary process of salvation.

Adam and Eve were created at different times to fulfill a divine design. I wish I could tell you with certainty what that design was. Nevertheless, I cannot. According to the Genesis account of Creation, God created every animal in pairs. However, He did not create Adam and Eve as a pair. Instead, He created Adam and when finished, God said, "It is not good for the man to be alone. I will make a helper suitable for him" (Gen. 2:18). What was missing in Adam's life was a suitable companion with whom he could share a lifetime of commitment, intimacy, and passion.

Without Eve, Adam had no one with whom he could share his love. Eve fulfilled the missing equation of God's design for Adam to experience passion, intimacy, pleasure, and procreation. God designed man and woman to live in pure intimacy, passion, and commitment when He said, "For this reason a man will leave his father and mother and be united to his wife, and they will become one flesh. The man and his wife were both naked, and they felt no shame" (Gen. 2:24–25). Eve became Adam's sexual partner for the text declares Adam united to his wife. He united with his Eve in total and perfect intimacy, free from fear, guilt, and shame.

It is God's plan for husbands to be appreciated by their wives

54

as refined men. He wants husbands to love, cherish, nourish, and complement their wives for the multifaceted functions they play in marriage.

The picture of wives revealed in the Bible is not one-dimensional. Frequently subjected to the rule of men, often adored for their beauty and purity, and occasionally praised for their leadership in times of crisis, women emerge from the pages of the Bible with as much complexity as men. Wives in biblical times lived in a patriarchal society.

Both the Old and New Testament worlds normally restricted the role of women primarily to the sphere of home and family, although a few strong women emerged as leaders. In religious life, women and children were subordinate to their husbands. A woman's father, husband, or other male relative usually gave her protection and direction.

Jesus opened the boundaries for women. He paid attention to them. His manner was inclusive as He acknowledged their place in the kingdom. He elevated the status of women by what He said and did. In addition, He affirmed the worth and value of women.

Paul also caught Jesus' vision. Although Paul faced the need to preserve order in the early church, he exclaimed in Galatians 3:28, "There is neither Jew nor Greek, slave nor free, male nor female, for you are all one in Christ Jesus." The final barrier preventing women from fully participating in the kingdom of God toppled under Jesus' influence.

The Old Testament shows women in more than one view. The predominant view is one of woman in subjection to man. However, at times, a woman was also the object of adoration and admiration. The Creation narrative in Genesis foreshadows two different perspectives regarding women. In Genesis 1:27, man and woman were created simultaneously in the thoughts of God. Woman, like man, is made in the image of God. Together, man and woman reflect the image of God. A woman was not in an inferior place in Creation, nor was she an afterthought of God.

Genesis 2:7–25 tells us man was created before woman, but in the account woman was viewed as being created for man as his helper. The account is often cited in support of the view that woman should remain subject to man since she had a subordinate position in Creation, but the narrative describes woman as a *suitable partner* for whom man leaves his father and mother.

The subordination of woman appears more clearly in a close reading of the Ten Commandments. The Commandments are addressed to men, a fact evidenced by the use of masculine pronouns. A major evidence of women's subordination is the reference to man not to covet any of his neighbor's property. His wife is included in the list of possessions. (See Exodus 20:17.)

Marriage and divorce were areas in which a woman's rights were subordinate to those of a man's. If a woman, who was about to be married, was suspected of not being a virgin, she was required to submit to a test. If the test proved she was not a virgin, she could be stoned to death at her father's door. (See Deuteronomy 22:13–21.) The requirement was not necessary for a man. If a man and woman were caught in the act of adultery, both of them were stoned. Adultery was a crime against the husband's rights, and the stoning vindicated those rights. (See Deuteronomy 22:22.)

If a jealous husband had questions about his wife's faithfulness, he could take her to the priest and have her submit to an intricate test to determine her guilt or innocence. (See Numbers 5:11–31.) However, if a wife suspected her husband of being unfaithful, she did not have the same right to confront her husband.

Divorce was always slanted toward the husband. He could obtain a divorce from his wife "Because he finds something indecent about her" (Deut. 24:1). The Jews variously interpreted the phrase "something indecent," and it ran the gamut from adultery to burned toast!

Inequity between boys and girls existed from the very beginning of life. A mother who bore a girl was considered unclean twice as long as a mother who bore a boy. During her time of purification, after the birth of her baby, a mother "must not touch anything sacred or go to the sanctuary until the days of her purification are over" (Lev. 12:4).

Proverbs 31 gives a picture of the hardworking, praiseworthy, "virtuous" woman. Yet, woman's most positive image was that of wife and mother. Against the predominant pattern of women in subordinate roles, several positive images emerged from the Old Testament. The birth of children was a sign of God's favor bestowed upon a woman. A particular sign of God's favor was the birth of male children. (See Genesis 29:31–30:24.) Her position as wife and mother undoubtedly venerated her.

The Ten Commandments cite a son's duty to honor both his father and mother. (See Exodus 20:12.) The ideal woman, eulogized in Proverbs 31, was a wife and mother who industriously fulfilled both roles, in addition to engaging profitably in the business world.

The story of Ruth is a good example of a traditional woman admired for her role as a good daughter-in-law. Ruth and Naomi, whose husbands died, were women of worth whom God aided by sending Boaz as their protector. (See Ruth 1:1–4:22.)

A thread that crosses the dominant pattern of the subjection of woman is one that depicts her positively. Wisdom, which held high value for the Hebrew people, was personified as "she" in Proverbs 1:20 and 7:4. The prophet Isaiah used a mother's love for her child as a model for God's love for His people in Isaiah 49:15 and 66:13. Several women—Miriam, Deborah, Huldah, and Esther—earned the respect and admiration of the Israelite nation by playing significant roles in times of national crisis.

A woman, as the other factor in a man's life, must be seen for who she is. Peter tells husbands they need to be "considerate as you live with your wives, and treat them with respect as the weaker partner and as heirs with you of the gracious gift of life…" (1 Pet. 3:7).

Looking at Jesus Christ our Lord and Master example of how He saw women will help us understand what Peter was saying in the text. Jesus recognized women to be weaker than men and to be more refined than men; He allowed them to minister to Him using their refined skills. It was a woman who was moved with compassion to anoint Him for His burial. Women, as the weaker vessel, could best be interpreted as being a more refined vessel.

Adam was made from the dust of the earth, but Eve was made from Adam's rib. As such, women need to be seen as a more refined vessel. As a more refined vessel women see things as a micro manager would. Whereas men see things as macro managers. Men see the big picture; whereas, women see the fine details. God designed the marital relationship to function with macro and micro managers, and neither is better than the other. Both personality types are needed to create a balance and wholeness in relationships.

Many scholars' interpretation of women as the weaker vessel is: anemic, impotent, frail, sick, and feeble. However, I do believe Peter was telling husbands they need to realize their wives are more interested in details and the fine art of things; as such, they should be respected and honored in those areas of life. Husbands need to understand their wives are designed to see the aesthetics of life, to reason that is more important than how they see things, and honor the difference. In general, husbands would be more interested in having a nice dinner; whereas, wives would be more interested in how the food is prepared and served. Wives are more interested in the refined details.

Women are weaker, more refined vessels, and husbands need to treat them with more care and understanding than how they would treat other men. Failing to do so will prevent a husband's prayer from being answered.

It behooves husbands, who are one in union with their wives, to show great love, respect, and appreciation to the make up and character of their wives. Jesus, having so much love for women as the weaker and more refined vessels, demonstrated that care on the cross. While suspended between heaven and earth, Jesus called on John to take care of His mother, Mary. "When Jesus therefore saw His mother, and the disciple standing by, whom he loved, he saith unto his mother, 'Woman, behold thy son!' Then saith he to the disciple, 'Behold thy mother!' And from that hour that disciple took her unto his own home" (John 19:26–27, KJV).

That was a small detail in comparison to what Jesus was doing and experiencing on the cross, but He took the time to see about His mother's care. It had nothing to do with the eternal plan of salvation, but it was important to Jesus. He understood how women think and feel, and as a result He saw to her welfare. I believe Mary appreciated the love Jesus shared on the cross. She was not left alone to fend for herself. Likewise, husbands need to understand the make up of their wives and treat them appropriately to maintain health in the marriage.

It is clear from Scripture the rib used to make woman made a difference. Today, women are still making a great contribution and difference in love and life when they are honored and respected for who God created them to be. If husbands will continue to love and cherish their wives, God will use women to make a difference for their families, churches, and communities at large.

## DISCUSSION

1. How did Jesus open the boundaries for women?

2. What are the two views of women mentioned in the Old Testament?

3. Discuss Genesis 1:27 and Genesis 2:7–25.

4. Discuss the role that tradition and culture play in the formation of women.

5. What is the definition of *helpmate*?

6. How influential were women to Jesus' ministry?

7. Are women actually the weaker vessel? Why or why not?

8. Did Jesus treat women as lesser human beings?

9. What is the common interpretation of weaker vessel?

10. What is the biblical understanding of weaker vessel?

*Chapter 6*

# MARRIAGE GLORY!

*But woman is the glory of man.*

—1 CORINTHIANS 11:7, KJV

O UR WORLD AND, it is sad to say, the church have become
so preoccupied with divorce and crisis in families that we
have failed to notice the good marriages that are around us from
which we can learn. We need to focus on the positives of marriage and seek ways to improve wounded marriage relationships
in order to avoid divorces.

Yes, the divorce statistics have painted nothing but doom and
gloom about marriage. In 2000 an estimated 49 percent of couples in the United States divorced. According to the same report,
in the Christian arena 54 percent of couples divorced, which is
an alarming number. That is fact. But, emphasizing the negatives
will not change the outcome.

The apostle Paul, writing in 1 Corinthians 7:11, said a man (husband), "Ought not to cover his head because man (husband) is the
image and glory of God: but the woman (wife) is the glory of the
man (husband)" (KJV). Paul continues, "Nevertheless, neither is
the man (husband) without the woman (wife), neither the woman
(wife) without the man, (husband) in the Lord. For as the woman
is of the man, even so is the man also by the woman; but all things
of God" (vv. 11–12). What Paul is declaring in his writing is marriages reflect the glory of God, the Author and Creator of humankind.

The Hebrew word for *glory* (*kabod*), in 1 Corinthian 11:7,
means "weight or worth." The worth or weight of marriage
comes from God to a husband and wife. As the husband reflects
the glory of God, the wife will reflect the glory as she receives it

through her husband. When husbands and wives are enjoying a harmonious marriage relationship they are reflecting the beauty and glory of God.

The glory or worth of marriage is reflected in the quality life and the relationship exemplified by husbands and wives.

Therefore, when a husband has weight he has worth, importance, and honor (glory). To describe a person as the glory of someone else is to define the person in terms of the one he or she reveals. When a husband is a man of God, he has weight and importance; he is the glory of God. He is a living demonstration or image of his Maker; therefore, he will love his wife as Christ loves the church. He will be willing to lay down his life for his wife as Christ laid down His life for the church, His bride.

Man, as the glory of God, reflects the image of God. In a similar way, when a woman has weight and importance, she reflects the (glory) weight, worth, or importance of her husband. When husbands and wives realize that their existence and worth are intertwined with each other, they will do all they can to help each person become the best they can be in their marital relationship.

The glory of God was seen upon Moses in a physical way. Likewise, I believe the glory of a happy marriage must be seen in physical ways at home and in the public life.

It can be seen through the level of commitment, passion, service, and intimacy expressed in marriage. Couples expecting to have happy and satisfying marriages, of worth and weight, need to maintain a high level of positivity, empathy, acceptance, love, and respect for each other. When those characteristics are present in a marriage, you can rest assure the glory of marriage will be attained.

The story recorded by Solomon in Proverbs 31 speaks of a virtuous woman. The virtuous woman had a husband who was a ruler in the community. He was a man of worth and weight whose wife also had the worth of her husband as she fulfilled her role as a virtuous woman. She was a reflection of the glory of her husband, so much so that even her children called her blessed.

A marriage of worth is one where couples love and work together in complementing each other, building a life, a work, or a ministry in which others can see their harmonious lives as a model to emulate.

Glory in marriage is not made overnight, but with unconditional love and respect, heavenly bliss is available for anyone in marriage who dares to allow the Spirit of God to be Lord of their relationship.

A wife is not powerless. She has delegated power to be used in the marriage union according to God's design in collaboration with her husband. A Christian husband should demonstrate a life of love to reflect the glory and image of God, and the wife should use her power to add significance to her husband and ultimately exalt their marriage.

Therefore, when they stand together at home or in public places, their presence should display the glory of God and demonstrate a loving relationship to those who look at them. As the glory of God was seen upon Moses in a physical way, so should the glory of a happy marriage union be seen in physical ways at home and in the public lives of each married person.

We have a choice—listen to the negative reports, or reflect on the positive reports of marriage and be influenced by them while building a glorious relationship.

We have covered many issues about women in the Bible, but there is one more crucial issue, and we will focus on it in the next chapter.

## DISCUSSION

1. What does the word *glory* mean?

2. Is this text applicable for husbands and wives today? If yes, why?

3. In what way is a husband the "glory of God"?

4. In what ways can wives be the "glory of man"?

5. Is a woman powerless in the marriage union?

6. In what ways does she have power?

7. How do couples reflect the glory of God?

## Chapter 7

## LOVING PARTNERSHIP

*Wives, submit to your husbands as to the Lord. For the
husband is the head of the wife as Christ is the head of
the church, his body, of which he is the Savior. Now as the
church submits to Christ, so also wives should submit to
their husbands in everything.*

—EPHESIANS 5:22–24

R EAL LOVE BLOOMS where there is mutual partnership. Good
marriages function on total partnership. Other types of
marital arrangements fall short of the full bliss that is available in
a marital relationship.

Marriage is a divine partnership of two whole people made in
the image of God. God endows each person in the partnership
with certain responsibilities and functions to fulfill the oneness
of marriage. Adam never knew real love until he was given his
wife Eve. Before Eve came along, Adam was single and lonely.
When he received Eve to be his wife, he quickly identified her as
an equal partner. He said she is "bone of my bones and flesh of my
flesh" (Gen. 2:23). He identified her as his soul mate with a womb
when he called her "woman." (See Genesis 2:23.) Adam and Eve
maintained a mutual partnership until death. They participated
in raising their family and served to provide for the needs amidst
family crisis and difficulties.

When I was a boy growing up, I often heard my mother talk
about my father as the breadwinner of the family. As the breadwinner, he was treated as king of the house. My mother would
sacrifice her own needs to keep him happy and well taken care
of. She would give him the best of every meal, because he was the
breadwinner. As a boy I resented that kind of treatment. Do not
misinterpret my thoughts. I loved my father. He was a great dad
to the family and me. He was a great servant of God, God rest his
soul. The problem I had was seeing him as the sole breadwinner
and how he was treated.

I believe it is a myth to think the sole breadwinner is the one who earns the money to take care of the family. I viewed both parents as breadwinners. In my eyes, both parents were mutual partners in the breadwinning process.

Indeed, my father was the only one earning money to care for the family needs. However, I believe breadwinning also means monies earned and monies saved. There was no way for my father to raise enough money to take care of thirteen children and meet all the needs of his family. My mom, as a loving partner, worked with him to manage the little money he earned and saved enough to meet our needs. If my father had to pay for babysitting, pay someone to clean the house, and cook for the family, there is no way we would be alive today. My mom helped him by serving as a loving mother, housekeeper, wife, and everything in the home. Whether both spouses work outside the home, or one works outside the home and the other stays home, they are both breadwinners. For too long, little thought has been given to stay-at-home parents—it is as if they are just housekeepers. No, they are breadwinners. They are helping to keep more bread in the family, and their job at home must be valued equally with the person working outside the home. Both husbands and wives need to be valued as mutual partners in the bread-winning process. However, that is a problem regarding marital partnership.

Another problem Christians have with marital relationships is they miss the message God intended when He set up the hierarchy husbands and wives are called to serve. Each partner in marriage needs to function as the Word of God dictates if they are going to fulfill the highest good and the maximum love each person can experience.

## Mutual Submission

One of the most controversial topics among the secular and religious worlds today is the issue of submission and headship in marriage. It is a topic of which discussion must continue if marriage in the twenty-first century is going to rebound and reverse the high divorce rates. For years, the religious world has debated those topics and by doing so have missed the bigger picture of God's arrangement.

In 1999, when the Southern Baptist Convention met in Oklahoma, they amended their declaration of beliefs to assert that a wife should "{submit graciously to the servant leadership of her husband." Because of the act, the secular media ridiculed the SBC. The reality of it is the declaration reaffirmed the biblical genre of subjection in marriage as God's standard and order. Many female liberal theologians and feminists are speaking out against the biblical order, but we must remember God made the world and He has the right to determine its order and operation.

When we learn to follow God's careful design and order of creation, we will experience divine harmony and earthly bliss. Wives are expected to submit to their husbands subsequent to the expression of their love. God designed the order, but God's design is not the problem with marriage—it is mankind's abuse of God's order. If husbands are commanded to love their wives, husbands and wives must learn how to submit to each other in the Lord, and out of the same spirit, wives should follow the divine order of submission.

There have been different interpretations of the roles of husbands and wives in marriage. There is neither male nor female, for you are all one in Christ Jesus. (See Galatians 3:28.) Human sexuality (maleness or femaleness) is an important aspect of human personality. (See Genesis 1:27.)

The Bible provides considerable support for traditional roles of husbands and wives, and it also provides examples of a variety of male/female roles. Martha performed a traditional role by preparing a meal for guests, but Mary played the nontraditional role of learner. (See Luke 10:38–42.) Esau was a hunter, but Jacob liked to cook. (See Genesis 25:27–29.) Leaders in the home and in society were generally men, but there were exceptions. Deborah was a judge. (See Judges 4–5.) Lydia was a merchant. (See Acts 16:14.)

Priscilla and Aquilla seemed to have acted as a team in teaching Apollos. (See Acts 18:26.) They also provided a meeting place for the church. (See Romans 16:3–5; 1 Corinthians 16:19.) Even the ideal wife in Proverbs 31 exercised considerable creativity and initiative in far-ranging projects. (See Proverbs 31:16–20.)

Different interpretations exist about authority and submission in marriage. On the one hand, there are those who believe that the husband, as head of the house, has a delegated authority from God over his wife. In that view, the wife's response is submission. On the other hand, there are those who believe in a model of a modern kind. They see a democratic marriage, one in which the partners are equal in every sense of the word. In between are Christians who advocate a mutual submission in love as the ideal but also believe the husband has special leadership responsibilities. The key biblical passages in the debate are Ephesians 5:21–32; Colossians 3:18–19; and 1 Peter 3:1–7. Advocates of strong male authority interpret those passages in light of the various biblical passages as reflecting the husband's authority. (See 1 Corinthians 14:34–35; 1 Timothy 2:11–14.)

Those who take a more moderate view make the following points: Jesus' actions gave women a higher status than was accorded by the society of His day. (See Luke 8:1–3; 10:38–42; John 4:7–30.) Paul's more idealistic statements and actual practice indicate that his harder teachings may have been conditioned by specific situations in some first-century churches. (See Galatians 3:28; Acts 16:14–15; Romans 16:3–6.)

The admonition to mutual submission in Ephesians 5:21 applies to all the relationships within the church and in a Christian marriage. (See Ephesians 5:21–33; 5:25–6:10.) Paul and Peter both use submission to refer to voluntary submission in a loving relationship, not the forced subjugation under an authority such as in a military organization. The biblical references say to submit yourself to one another, not to put the other person under your subjection. (See Ephesians 5:21–22, 24; Colossians 3:18; 1 Peter 3:1.) In that type of relationship, the husband's role as head is modeled after the self-giving of Christ. (See Ephesians 5:23, 25; Philippians 2:1–11; 1 Peter 3:7.)

The apostle Paul's passages on marriage, found in Colossians 3:18–19; Ephesians 5:22–23, and 1 Peter 3:1, speak of women in submission to their husbands. It is therefore important to notice the significant role the concept of subjection or submissiveness plays in the New Testament.

Before we conclude, it is important to state that nowhere in the Bible does submission in marriage mean inferiority. Christ Himself submitted to the Father in 1 Corinthians 15:28. The submission in those passages has to do with obeying one's calling, being subject to the demands of the office. Nowhere does it state women are to be subject to men. However, in the position of wife, a woman is to lovingly submit herself to her husband's love, care, and leadership. They submit one to another in the fear of God.

Paul's call to submission is important because he tells wives to submit to their own husbands. Submitting to one another does not involve being substandard; instead, it is the calling to serve each other in order to fulfill God's will. Thus, Paul does not imply women are deficient or inferior even when he reminds wives to submit to their husbands in Ephesians 5:22, "Wives, submit to your husbands as to the Lord"; or Colossians 3:18, "Wives, submit to your husbands, as is fitting in the Lord."

Moreover, the focus is not so much on the wives and husbands as it is on the offices of wives and husbands as they relate to each other. In effect, Paul is saying, "Be wives as is fitting in the Lord," that is, as the norm for marriage instructs and God requires.

The knowledge of marriage relations is especially striking when we see that in Ephesians 5:25 Paul immediately adds, "Husbands, love your wives, just as Christ loved the church and gave himself up for her." In Colossians 3:19 he continues, "Husbands, love your wives and do not be harsh with them." Paul is saying, "Remember what Christ did for the church. The care He showed is the care you should share in your marriages."

Although the wives may have some legitimate grievances, the solution is neither running away nor a writ of divorce. Even as Paul instructs wives to be good wives, he exhorts husbands to be good husbands. Both husbands and wives are to live up to their calling. She is to be a loving and submissive wife, and he is to be a loving, caring, and gentle husband.

We must not conclude that women do not have to submit to or love their husbands, nor should we believe husbands do not have to love or care for their wives. That conclusion would be preposterous. Paul is calling both husbands and wives to be obedient to the standards of marriage, which involve mutual love and mutual submission. The equality of marriage is heightened even more when we recall that in Christ's life, submission and love were synonymous—to love was to serve. Christ emphasized the service concept of marriage in direct contrast to the other concepts in existence at the time. Six times in the Gospels we read the greatest must is to be the servant of all. (See Matthew 20:26–28; 23:11; Mark 9:3–5; 10:43, 45; Luke 9:48; 22:26–27.) Naturally, then, Christ requires husbands and wives to submit to each other in love and thus obey the will of God.

First Peter 3:1 deserves mention because, in an indirect way, it confirms our contention that being in subjection does not mean being "bossed around." Wives are to be in subjugation to their husbands so that if any man is an unbeliever, he can perhaps be won for Christ by the behavior of his wife. That subjection, however, does not entail authority to forbid wives from believing in Christ. Like Paul, Peter called wives and husbands to function as mandated.

Christianity should make it easier for a husband to love his wife. However, religion does not set the standard for love. God is love, and He establishes love and places it in an intimate union. He also places the responsibility of maintaining and sustaining that love on the shoulder of the husband, whether he is a Christian or not. Wives, according to Peter, are not to be show-offs or to play the role of the "loose" woman. Likewise, husbands are to act with understanding and to love their wives as vessels designed to be loved. (See 1 Peter 3:7.)

What is the duty of the Christian husband? The Scriptures are clear in that regard. He is to live with his wife, and he is to understand and honor her with the highest esteem.

The Greek word *sunoikein* means to dwell with, to remain with, or to reside with. Husbands are to remain with their wives and treat them with love, knowing they are heirs together of the same grace of life. (See 1 Peter 3:7.) Many believe sunoikein means sexual intercourse. It is similar to the Hebrew verb for "to know" which means a man and woman know each other sexually. The point is the husband has to dwell with his wife and no one else. He is to dwell with her in purity, righteousness, and holiness—not be an adulterer.

To dwell with his wife also means the husband is not to be gone all the time pursuing his own interests and hobbies. A good husband dwells at home, he is close to his wife, and he is supportive of her in all aspects of her life. The husband and wife are a team. They are as one body; one body that lives and moves together. That will not do away with individuality because individuality never has been and never will be the problem within a marriage. Individuality complements marriage. Husbands and wives must always remember this: they are to live their lives thinking of ways to constantly improve the mutuality and individuality of marriage relationships.

> For this cause shall a man leave his father and mother, and cleave to his wife; and they twain shall be one flesh: so then they are no more twain, but one flesh. What therefore God hath joined together, let not man put asunder.
> —MARK 10:7–9, KJV

> And Adam said, This is now bone of my bones, and flesh of my flesh: she shall be called Woman, because she was taken out of Man. Therefore shall a man leave his father and his mother, and shall cleave unto his wife: and they shall be one flesh.
> —GENESIS 2:23–24, KJV

Husbands are to live with their wives in knowledge. That is a fact too often ignored and neglected. However, the Scripture is clear. A husband is not to be ignorant in living with his wife. He is to know and understand:

- The marriage relationship—what marriage is and what it is to be
- His wife—her nature and emotional makeup; what she needs and wants emotionally and spiritually; her strengths and weaknesses
- His duties—what the Word of God says

A husband knows and understands his wife. He should not be prejudiced and inconsiderate, blind and close-minded, or a detached and inconsiderate observer.

In a simple, pointed way Matthew Henry said in his *Commentary*, "Husbands are to dwell with the wife according to knowledge; not according to lust, as brutes; nor according to passion, as devils; but according to knowledge, as wise and sober men, who know the Word of God and their own duty."[1]

Husbands and wives are admonished in Scriptures to honor each other. The Greek word for *honor* (*timen*) means to value, to esteem, to prize, to count as precious. Spouses are to count each other as precious gems, a prize of extreme value. They are to highly esteem the other.

The husband is to honor his wife as the weaker vessel. Wives are to honor her husband as the source of her love. By nature, the wife is more delicate. That means the husband has to:

- Protect her
- Be the primary provider
- Assume leadership in the home
- Oversee the family and its welfare

Husbands are to look after and care for their wives with warmth and tenderness, treating them in the most precious of spirits. In return wives should receive their husbands love and care out of a benevolent spirit. They should not see this tenderness as weakness, but instead, honor their desire to create an environment that will cause them to be more fulfilled in their marriage.

> Husbands, love your wives, even as Christ also loved the church, and gave himself for it.
> —Ephesians 5:25, kjv

In God's eyes, men and women are joint (equal) heirs. The husband is to honor his wife as a joint heir of the grace of life. The husband is neither above the wife nor the wife above the husband. God has no favorites. Spiritual gifts and rights are given to wives and husbands equally. Women receive the spiritual gifts of God just as men do.

Failure to honor the wife hinders the prayers of a husband. God will not answer the prayers of any husband who dishonors his wife. God hears the sighs of the wife, not the prayers of a mean and domineering husband. God is going to hear the broken and contrite heart, not the prayers of an arrogant and dominating spirit. Both husband and wife must love one another and live as God says to live, both fulfilling their duty to one another, if they wish God to answer their prayers.

> If I regard iniquity in my heart, the Lord will not hear me.
> —PSALM 66:18, KJV

> But your iniquities have separated between you and your God, and your sins have hid his face from you, that he will not hear.
> —ISAIAH 59:2, KJV

That does not mean the husband should always be in control. Paul stressed the equality of the roles. Recognizing their places as wife and husband, the partners must do everything in accordance with the biblical truths. Thus, Paul stated that even as the church is subject to Christ and she is not her own savior, so a wife is not to forget her role, but she is to be wife to her husband in everything. (See Ephesians 5:23.)

Look at Paul's teaching on the mutuality of marriage in 1 Corinthians 7:3–4, "The husband should fulfill his marital duty to his wife, and likewise the wife to her husband. The wife's body does not belong to her alone but also to her husband. In the same way, the husband's body does not belong to him alone but also to his wife." Here it is spelled out for us. There must be mutuality in the marital sexual relationship in order for love to be fully experienced. Wives and husbands should give themselves to their spouses, not necessarily by feelings, but should be motivated by the other's desire.

There are many different ways of expressing love. Although there are different roles established for the sexes in different cultures of the world, the command of God for man to love his wife crosses every culture and age. The church must now look at theology through some broader views such as the feminist, woman, black, poor, and the oppressed to balance out the Anglo-male, middle-class view of theology. The church is challenged to create a mosaic theology that does justice to all of mankind and to remain consistence with the Bible.

It is difficult to look at submission without looking at the incarnation of Jesus, because it epitomizes the submission and headship concept. In Philippians 2:1–11, we find the incarnation of Jesus Christ the truest representation of love and submission in action. If marriages are going to last, wives must practice the submissiveness demonstrated and practiced by Jesus Christ, and husbands must practice a loving leadership as God did with Jesus while He lived on this world.

Jesus Christ is the supreme example of submissiveness and humility. The above-mentioned passage says Jesus Christ is God, yet He humbled and submitted Himself to become man. Jesus Christ is the Person who dwelt in all the glory of perfection, but He humbled Himself and came to this corruptible world that was filled with selfishness, greed, and death. Jesus took an enormous step down to become a man. It will take the mind of Christ dwelling in a wife in order for her to submit to her husband, just as it will for the husband to love his wife according to the biblical standard.

When Paul made this statement in Philippians 2:6, "Who, being in very nature of God, did not consider equality with God something to be grasped," he made it clear Christ was the nature of God. Hence, Christ was fully God as He was fully man.

Jesus Christ is of the being of God. The Greek word for *being* (*huparchon*) means "existence," what a person is from within and without. It is the very essence of a person—what they are inside—that cannot be changed. It is who a person is and all they are. Jesus Christ is in the form of God. The Greek word for *form* (*morphe*) means "the permanent, constant being of a person." In contrast, it means the fleeting, outward form of a person that is always changing. For example, a man is always changing (*schema*) in looks because of age and fashion. However, his manhood (*morphe*) never changes.

In the incarnation, Jesus Christ emptied Himself and became a man. He, who existed in eternity and perfection, in glory and majesty, and in dominion and power, stepped down and became a man. But more so, He who was the Lord and Master of the universe who deserved all the honor and service of all living creatures took upon Himself the form of a servant. He became the servant of men—not only of God.

Jesus Christ made Himself of no reputation. That is, He emptied Himself. The Greek word for *emptied* (*ekenosen*) means "to completely empty." It is the picture of pouring water out of a glass until it is empty—dumping everything until it is all removed.

Matthew Henry made a brief but excellent statement about that fact, "He emptied Himself, divested Himself of the honors and glories of the upper world, and of His former appearance, to clothe Himself with the rags of human nature."[2]

When a wife submits to her husband in love, she is not giving up her essence or personhood. She is simply submitting herself to her husband in love, knowing he will love and care for her. Together they will be able to maximize each other—to fulfill their potential. When a wife fully submits to her husband and the husband fully gives unto his wife, the marriage will be modeled and emulated. If Christ, being God, could willingly submit to His father in love, then the same Christ, who indwells us and demonstrated how to submit and to love, will lead us to fulfill our roles. All we have to do is allow Him to guide us.

There is submission and unity in the Godhead (see Figure 1). Christ submitted to the Father and willingly came to earth to die for mankind. (See Mark 14:36.) The Holy Spirit came and fulfilled the promise of the Father in John 14:26. The Father submits to the advocacy of His Son as He intercedes for the church. (See John 17:9–26.)

## SUBMISSION IN THE GODHEAD

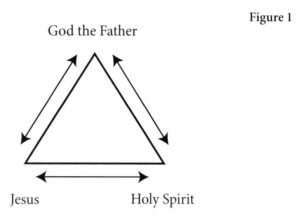

**Figure 1**

God the Father

Jesus           Holy Spirit

In Figure 2, the husband submits to Christ and the Holy Spirit infills them. In love, the husband leads his wife and she willingly submits to follow his leading. When the wife submits to her husband, she is also submitting to the divine design of Christ's norm for marriage. Wives are required to submit to their husbands as their husbands submit to God. (See Ephesians 5:21.)

## SUBMISSION OF HUSBAND AND WIFE TO GOD

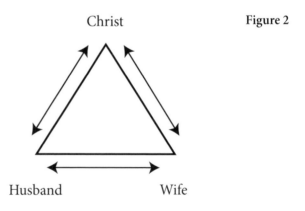

Christ

**Figure 2**

Husband           Wife

Marriage requires mutual submission between husbands and wives as they also submit to Christ, the head of the church—

the source of creation for mankind.

A spirit-filled husband will submit to Christ and out of his allegiance to Christ will pour forth his love to his wife. The wife in response submits to Christ and to the loving care and leadership of her husband. Love and submission work harmoniously as both submit to the divine leadership of Christ. There should not be one without the other.

## Who is the Real Boss?

Many Christian marriages are functioning at a mediocre love level because of the misunderstanding and misinterpretation of headship in marriage. Our culture is more interested in who has the final words in marriage, who is the real boss, rather than finding a blueprint to coordinate and navigate relationships in the institution of marriage. If husbands and wives are going to appreciate the love God has for them in their marriage, they need to understand God's structure for marriage and the implications of headship and submission. Couples must understand through careful study of the Word of God and not through their cultural, theological, and sociological presuppositions.

Wives need to know what to expect from their husbands, as head of their lives, based on the Word of God, and not by those same predispositions. As the head, husbands need to see their wives as a part of the marriage partnership.

A head is not good without a neck. The head and the neck need to work together if it is going to be of use to the other parts of the body. You cannot have one without the other. They are inseparable if they are to function and fulfill their designed roles.

Wives in the twenty-first century are looking for their husbands, their knights who swept them away with love, to care for them as their loving head and partner.

Too many Christian marriages are hurting because many husbands are functioning as authoritarian leaders rather than loving heads. Authoritarian leadership styles produce forced submission, but loving leadership produces volunteer submission in marriage.

A divine influence on the world will result in a series: God is the head of Christ, Christ is the head of man, man is the head of woman, and as such husbands are to love and care for their wives as Christ does the church—His bride. (See 1 Corinthians 11:3.) If we conclude from this passage that man is superior to woman, we must likewise conclude Christ is subordinate to God and also inferior. The church has denied the second conclusion, and it is time she emphatically rejects the first.

Christ is the head of the church, and as head, He has the power to do with the church whatever He chooses. However, we see Christ choose to function as the loving head of the church and the model of love for Christian husbands toward their wives. If husbands are to love their wives, as the Bible teaches, they must first understand their God-given loving position of "headship."

Many husbands and wives, through faulty understanding of God's Word and their cultural, theological, and sociological presuppositions, have been living beneath God's wonderful grace of love. Husbands and wives need to know what is expected of them through the loving dynamics of the headship in marriage relationships. A breakdown in the understanding has caused undue stress on marriage and has resulted in many marriages ending in divorce.

The biggest problem with the interpretation of headship is the emphasis is placed on one of its meanings. Most interpretations focus on the authority implied by the head rather than on the function. Being the head of one's wife does not really have anything to do with control, power, or authority, but it has everything to do with love—agape, unconditional love.

In the Old and New Testaments' usage, the word *head* often has the meaning of "source" or "beginning." The conservative Christian community has agreed the best rendition of the word would be "source," or something similar to our words *fountainhead* or *headwaters*. Therefore, a husband is the "source of his wife" (Eph. 5:23). The wife is a product of her husband. As Adam was the source from which Eve was made, likewise husbands are regarded as the source from which their wives come. As the source of his wife, he is moved to show love and care for his wife as he would love and care for his very own body.

A distinctive theological use of the word *head* was seen in the

New Testament concept of the "headship" of Christ. Christ is the head "source" (*kephale*-Greek) of His church and the church is His "bride." (See Ephesians 5:23–33.) In His role as "head" or source, Christ enables the church to grow, knits her into unity, nourishes her by caring for each member, and gives her strength to build herself up in love. (See Ephesians 4:15–16).

As the "loving head" of the church, Christ nourishes, purifies, cares for, and supplies the needs of the church. A husband, as the head, is expected to nourish, care for, and supply the needs of his wife. So many marriages are hurting and suffering today because of the lack of love. Many marriages are calling out for a fresh touch from a loving head. Too many marriages are love starved, and God is calling husbands to be the loving heads of their homes. Husbands are the source of God's love, and it is designed to flow to the wife and children.

As human beings we often times take time to nurture and plan for growth in various areas of our lives, but not marriage. It is time for husbands and wives to nurture and plan for growth of love in marriages. It will not happen by osmosis or wishing. Love will only grow where there is a conscious effort and plan to make love deposits. When love deposits are made in a relationship, it raises the love levels to emotional highs that produce or create ecstasy, excitement, or euphoria. Marriages are guaranteed to be lasting when husbands lead their loving wives as the loving head of their family.

Jesus initiates continuing, unceasing, loving actions toward His bride—the church. Daily, He cultivates the church through His loving care. Husbands, as the source of their wives must initiate continuing and unceasing loving actions toward their wives. In return, wives must respond to the loving actions of their husbands with reciprocal actions and respect.

As husbands, or "house-bands," God has given men the responsibility and authority to bind their households together. The band to use is love. Using Christ as the model and example, a husband is to be the loving head of his wife. They are to be the source, the initiator, and the instigator of love to the mate.

Wives, as the church voluntarily responds to the loving

actions initiated by Jesus Christ, you are freed by your husband's Christ-like attitude to respond to him with love, respect, and submission.

How can we integrate the concept of authority in headship and source of love? I do not need authority to love Jenny, my wife. She is my wife, and I am commanded to love her. (See Ephesians 5:25.) Loving her is both a responsibility and joy. If my love is to be expressed in words and deeds, I must have the authority in the form of her willingness to accept my love. She must authorize me or give me the power to love her. She must actualize my freedom to love her through a spirit of voluntary submission expressed in a willingness to be loved.

Christian wives should see their husbands as the loving head in their marriages and as such, husbands need to know their love is measurable, tangible, attainable, and a manageable expression of Jesus Christ. As mates grow in their love for Jesus Christ, they should grant permission to each other to demonstrate love more fully toward one another. Christian husbands must choose to be a loving head in order to fulfill God's order in marriage. Living by any other order will limit the full flow of love designed for each in marriage.

Christianity teaches God and Christ are equal in the Godhead. They are equal partners. However, each person in the Godhead plays different roles in the cosmos story.

The Genesis account of Adam and Eve's creation revealed they were created equally. In the Second Adam, Christ's equality was restored. However, in light of the God-created order of the family, man is the head because woman came from the man. Therefore, as the head, he is responsible for the welfare of his wife and family. Husbands are responsible for providing a loving environment for the well-being of his wife and children, just as Christ, the head of the church, provides for the loving environment and well-being of the church. It is clear from Scripture man is the head. However, husbands need to remember their wives are the neck that turns the head. Marriage is a partnership, and we need to function in our God-given roles to fulfill the marriage bliss. It is out of that loving headship that wives shine as the glory of their husbands.

## DISCUSSION

1. Discuss the traditional roles of husbands and wives.

2. Discuss some of the different interpretations of authority and submission in marriage.

3. Discuss how Christianity makes it easier for husbands and wives to function as a couple.

4. Discuss how Jesus demonstrated submission to the Father.

5. How does the submission of the church to Christ relate to a wife's submission in marriage?

6. Why do you believe God gave a hierarchical structure in the marriage union?

7. Based on the Word of God, what should wives expect from husbands?

8. How is the word *head* used in the New Testament in relation to Christ and husbands?

9. Should husbands create the lead in the home for providing a loving environment? If yes, how should it be done?

10. How should love be demonstrated in the headship of husbands?

11. How do you reconcile headship and mutual submission as taught in Scripture?

*Chapter 8*

# SILENCING LOVE

*Husbands, in the same way be considerate as you live with*
*your wives, and treat them with respect.*
—1 PETER 3:7, NIV

M Y WIFE AND I were transferred from Toronto, where I
served as a youth and christian education director, to the
Cathedral of Praise Church of God in Bridgeport, Connecticut.
Shortly after I left the Toronto church, my wife became pregnant
with our second child, Aleah. My wife would remain in Canada
until the baby was born.

One day, I decided to take my seven-year-old son with me to
visit my wife. I gave Jenny a call before we left to let her know we
were coming. Intuitively, Jenny asked, "By the way, what are you
driving to come here?"

I hesitated a little and then said, "My car, of course."

She exclaimed, "Do not use that old car of yours to bring my
son with you when you come to visit me."

"That old car," as she so delicately put it, was my thirteen-year-
old, fully loaded, 1980 Mercedes-Benz that had a wonderful inte-
rior and excellent body. I was convinced it was a good car and it
would take me anywhere I wanted to go, so I ignored her advice.

I went to church that Sunday night, preached, and immediately
after the service, I jumped into the car with my son and headed
for Toronto. Approximately three hours away from Bridgeport,
the clutch failed. I rented a hotel room for the night with my son
and the following morning had the car towed back to Bridgeport.
I finally made it to Toronto to visit my wife, but not without being
scolded. You would think that once bitten I would shy away from
such a childlike attitude, but I had not learned my lesson.

On the day I was to bring Jenny and Aleah back to Bridgeport,

I rented a car for the trip. When I arrived at the rental car office, they did not have the size car I had reserved. So, since my Mercedes-Benz was a bigger car, and it had undergone some major repairs, I decided it would be a better car to use to bring my family back home. Deja vu!

After I went to church and preached, my son and I jumped in the car and headed to Toronto. The night was very cold and over five feet of snow had accumulated on Highway 90 through Massachusetts. I left church and decided to gas up and service my vehicle. As I drove along listening to some gospel music, with my son sound asleep, I heard an unusual noise and stopped to see what it was. Since I am not mechanically inclined, I got right back into the car and decided to drive slowly to the next service station.

Well, you guessed it! The car broke down at the same spot it did on the first trip to Toronto. However, with God's sense of humor and His love for His children, He touched the heart of a tractor-trailer driver traveling to Niagara Falls to pick us up. He took us to the next service station, and once again, I rented a hotel room for the night. The following morning I had the car towed back to Bridgeport. I rented another car and headed to Toronto. After that, I made a pledge to never ignore the advice of my wife—even when I do not understand it. Her sharing of her thoughts, ideas, and opinions has been one of the great blessings to our marriage.

As the above story indicates, God designed men and women to function at different wavelengths. They each need the input of the other to completely fulfill God's design and operation for the marriage. The sooner husbands and wives take advantage of each other's brains and talents, the better their outcome in marriage and life will be.

There are many religious groups where women are not allowed to use their talents and knowledge, and sometimes the same principle is transferred to their home life. God is interested in marriages working in harmony. He has set up laws to govern marriage. When these laws are ignored, subverted, broken, or destroyed, love will be silenced, abused, or even die.

Christian marriages have been suffering because of a lack

of communication that can be traced back to some of our mis-interpreted scriptural beliefs. The sooner we align our beliefs with God's intended meaning, we will see obvious differences in our marriages.

I have counseled many couples in which wives were not allowed to speak their minds on any issues. If they did, the husbands felt that the wives needed to be silenced. (In the rare case did I encounter a wife who felt the husband needed to be silent.) These Christian husbands feel threatened, and they say that when their wives speak they are disrespecting them. Sometimes this is true, but in most cases this is not so. These husbands are saying their wives need to learn how to keep silent. Some of these husbands apply Paul's teaching on women's silence in the church to their marriages. Issues in marriage must be addressed with mutual respect and love; silence is not the answer. Each person must be given the opportunity to lovingly express his or her opinions without feeling belittled or restrained by faulty scriptural teaching. Avoiding the pain that comes with the problem tends to lead to abuse in marriage.

Paul never intended his teaching about women keeping silent in church to apply to marriage. Instead, Paul argues that "women should remain silent in the churches. They are not allowed to speak, but must be in submission, as the Law says. If they want to inquire about something, they should ask their husbands at home; for it is disgraceful for a woman to speak in the church" (1 Cor. 14:34–35).

Often commentators assume that subordinate means subordinate to man. That is an unfounded assumption because that is not what the text says.

It is presumptuous to claim, as many do, that when Paul referred to the law, he was referring to Genesis 3:16. Is it reasonable to assume he made special reference to the Creation story as he did in 1 Timothy 2:13–14? When we take Paul's words in their full context, the meaning is something like this: "women, you are not above the law; you too are under obedience as the law directs, but since you are abdicating your lawful office of coworker with man, you should keep quiet."

Since Paul connected the silence of women with their desire to learn, it appears he was warning women that they were speaking out of ignorance, and he was admonishing them to ask their husbands if they had questions. (See 1 Corinthians 14:35.) Paul's prohibition was against their unprofitable interruptions in the assemblies. His stringent measures must also be understood.

Teaching women in the synagogues was completely foreign to Jewish law. Paul was not forbidding all participation of women in worship services, but he *was* forbidding women to speak in the part of the service involving dialogue-type discussion. Then the women were apparently at their bickering best, trying to embarrass, if not defy, their husbands. To stop such confusing spectacles, " . . . so that the church may be edified. . . . For God is not a God of disorder but of peace," Paul issued an edict calling women to task (1 Cor. 14:5, 33). He is not deriding them, but urging them to obey their calling as women.

The usual interpretation is Paul's forbidding all feminine participation in worship services. As a result of faulty interpretation, many men have transferred the same principle to their marriage, and do not allow their wives to use their gifts in the marriage union. When we study Paul's teaching, we find those same men faced another problem—they realized Paul allowed women to prophesy and to pray. (See 1 Corinthians 11:5.)

God has given women beauty and brains, and the sooner husbands recognize those wonderful blessings and begin to use them, the fuller the marriage union will become. If women are allowed to pray and prophesy in church, they were designed to be used of God in their marriage union without being hindered by faulty theological interpretations

In many ways, 1 Timothy chapter 2 intensifies 1 Corinthians chapter 14, "A woman should learn in quietness and full submission. I do not permit a woman to teach or to have authority over a man; she must be silent" (1 Tim. 2:11–12). Paul was upset by the disturbing antics of women in the congregation. In a construction corresponding to 1 Corinthians 14, Paul commands women to be silent and to learn subjection. Again, it is important to note the text does not read "submission to men."

Apparently, it was like the situation in Corinth; women were interrupting the services to embarrass and perhaps dominate their husbands and other men. It is worth noting Paul does not say women cannot exercise authority over men; instead, women are not to dominate men and dictate (*authentien*-Greek) to them. In so doing, women break their partnership relation with men and usurp God's authority over men, as well as women.

Paul insists women learn they are to be helpmates for men, subject to God's will for women and not competitors aiming to dominate. Humankind's trouble began when Eve set aside her partnership role with man under God. She was deceived, then proceeded to dominate man and lead him astray.

Paul's call for silence was a short-term solution to the problem that was in the Corinthian church. The call was given so that he could reestablish order. He then he proceeded to explain that there must be harmony in business meetings, and that husbands and wives need to work out their differences at home and come to the public meeting in harmony. He wanted things to be done according to order.

Throughout Scripture, we see God using a woman's beauty and brains in ministry and marriage according to order. Esther was a beautiful woman. "She had neither father nor mother, and the maid was fair and beautiful…" (Esther 2:7, KJV). Esther was selected to be the wife of, and queen to, King Ahasuerus. "So Esther was taken unto King Ahasuerus into his house royal….And the king loved Esther above all the women, and she obtained grace and favor in his sight more than all the virgins; so that he set the royal crown upon her head, and made her queen instead of Vashti" (vv. 16–17).

Queen Esther realized she was made queen for a special reason, not only because she was beautiful, but also because she had a brain that God could use. Her life, the lives of her people, and her husband's kingdom were threatened by the plan of Haman to have all the Jews of Sushan killed. But she used her brain and thwarted the plan of Naaman. Esther established divine order when she had the Jews fast for three days before she went to see the king. God honored her plan because she sought his will first. She established divine protocol. She went under the protection and guidance of God. As a result her life, her people's lives, and her husband's kingdom were not destroyed. If Esther had not sought and received the favor of God, she would not have received the favor of the king. God's favor caused Ahasuerus to grant her favor and audience.

Let us look at another courageous woman in Proverbs 31. The text is constantly read and used in religious and civic circles when speaking about mothers and women. The text reveals the story of a beautiful and brilliant woman. "Who can find a virtuous woman? For her price is far above rubies" (Prov. 31:10, KJV). The writer went on to describe her: "She openeth her mouth with wisdom; and in her tongue is the law of kindness. She looketh well to the ways of her household, and eateth not the bread of idleness. Her children arise up, and call her blessed; her husband also, and he praiseth her. Many daughters have done virtuously, but thou excellest them all" (Prov. 31:26–29, KJV). She is given talents to enhance her family; her children, her husband, and her community speak well of her.

A woman, who uses her brain and beauty to enhance her family and elevate her husband, strengthens her marriage bond and minimizes the possibility of divorce. The Bible is filled with stories where the beauty and brains of women are used to fulfill His design in marriage. These stories contradict the seemingly prescriptive issue of wives and silence in marriage or the church. If Esther had kept silent, not only would Ahasuerus lose his beautiful wife, but he would also lose a good portion of his people and resources.

One problem with many relationships is that many husbands feel threatened when their wives use their initiative or creativity in trying to solve a problem. Those issues, plus some husbands' insecurity and poor self-esteem, lead them to become abusive to their wives, which not only silences their love, but, for some, wounds it for life.

Couples enter the marriage relationship as whole persons, and they must be accepted and treated as such. Whenever the wholeness is threatened, abuse will enter. When husbands misuse

Scripture or abuse power to control their wives, they are wounding and silencing love.

Domestic abuse is another silencer of love and another reason for the rise in divorce rates. It must be removed from homes if love is going to flourish there. Domestic abuse is often used in a relationship when words alone cannot articulate one's thoughts and feelings or when these words are not obeyed.

Domestic abuse is a major social issue for today's marriages and society as well as for the church. Family violence, while common around the world, is not a universal problem. It is rare or nonexistent in only 15 percent of societies. However, David Levinson in, *Family Violence in Cross-Cultural Perspective,* stated the factors that influence low, or no, family violence include monogamous marriages, economic equality between the sexes, equal access to divorce by men and women, the availability of alternative caretakers for children, and frequent and regular intervention by neighbors and family in domestic disputes.[1]

Loving couples need to raise the standard for husband–wife relationships and should challenge husbands or wives who abuse each other to cease the abusive behavior.

In 1985, husbands or boyfriends killed more than 1,300 women, or 30 percent of the total homicide rate for females, while wives or girlfriends killed 6 percent of male homicide victims. Approximately 37 percent of pregnant females across class, race, and educational lines are physically abused. Four million women are severely assaulted each year. More than one-third of assaults on women involve severe aggression such as punching, kicking, choking, or the use of a knife or gun. Some of these women were and are Christian wives. Lack of loving solutions will allow this evil behavior to continue unabated.

In her book, *A Journey Through Domestic Violence Every Eighteen Seconds,* Nancy Kilgore said from one-fifth to one-third of all women are physically assaulted by a partner in their lifetimes. Approximately 95 percent of battered victims are women, and 21 percent of all women who use hospital emergency services are abuse victims. The rate of injury to battered women surpasses that of car accidents and muggings combined.[2]

There are usually no exterior signs, no "marks of Cain," to distinguish the batterer. Abusers cut across all ethnic, religious, cultural, and professional lines. This fact is a strong and sobering rebuke to those who think batterers are only in poor urban areas of a certain race or class.

Abuse is not only a problem for wives. There are many reports made by husbands about the abuse they have received. It is not a result of what Rita-Lou Clarke states, in her *Pastoral Care of Battered Wives,* is a response to the husband's violence toward his wife. Sometimes, after suffering abuse for years, a wife will retaliate by becoming violent herself. She feels it is the only way she can protect herself and, perhaps, her children. Husband abuse is on the increase for many reasons; more research needs to be done on husband abuse.[3]

In a traditional marriage, the wife is more likely to be bound economically and socially. If she has children, the wife is doubly bound for she is the primary caregiver of the children.

The time has come for individuals living in abusive relationships to name the crisis—wife/husband abuse. Your marriage should be a haven. Marriage is designed for a loving relationship, and if there is abuse in the relationship couples will not be able to maximize their full potential.

The power of naming is the power of self-authorization. In order for a person to end his/her battering experience, he/she must first acknowledge that the behavior is evil and wrong. That is the first step. Silence protects the status quo, and the status quo favors the person who batters. Silence will only cause your problem to get worse. Get help as early as possible and minimize the effects of abuse.

Many researchers in the field of abuse consider the primary characteristic of batterers to be low self-esteem. According to the Rollo May book, *Power and Innocence,* in many cases those trying to establish their self-esteem do so by performing deeds of violence.[4]

Lenore Walker, a leading researcher in the field of battered women, produced the following description of batterers in her book, *The Battered Woman:*

> A batterer (usually male) has low self-esteem, believes all the myths about battering relationships; is a traditionalist, believes in male supremacy and the stereotypical masculine sex role in the family, blames others for action; is pathologically jealous, presents a dual personality, has severe stress reactions during which he uses (sic) drinking and wife battering to cope; frequently uses sex as an act of aggression to enhance self-esteem in view of waning virility; may be bisexual; does not believe his violent behaviors should have negative consequences.[5]

According to Ann Storr in her book, *Family Violence: An International and Interdisciplinary,* "It is the insecure and inadequate who most easily feel threatened, and who resort to violence as a primitive way of restoring dominance."[6]

I. M. and M. A. Allen agree in their writing, *Basics of Qualitative Research,* that "men who batter women have a strong need to preserve their egos while at the same time keep their women in check." A husband who feels his social status is inconsistent with social norms is more likely to use violence in dealing with his wife. For example, the woman who has more education or a better job than her male partner is at risk for wife beating if he has low self-esteem, and especially if he strongly believes in the prerogatives of male dominance. A woman should not be subjected to abuse just because she was born into wealth, or acquired a good education and subsequently a good job.[7]

Marriage is a partnership. Therefore, couples should realize that whatever they earn from their livelihood is to meet their needs, and it should not matter who earns the most. If there is a problem with who is earning the most, it is time to seek help with your marriage.

## THE CYCLE OF ABUSE

The cycle I am describing, first developed in Walker's *Battered Women,* has three phases—the tension-building phase, the acute-battering incident, and the kind-and-contrite loving behavior.

Walker contends, "Stress feeds the tension-building phase." The more stress you are under, the shorter the phase lasts, and the abuse that follows is more severe. That phase can last anywhere from days to several years. It is like a pressure cooker being placed over an open flame without a release valve. As the batterer and the battered sense the escalating tension during this first phase, it becomes more difficult for the coping techniques to work. Each becomes more frantic. The man or the woman increases his or her possessive smothering and brutality. His or her attempts at psychological humiliation become more barbed, and their verbal harangues are longer and more hostile. He or she hovers around barely giving the batterer room to breathe on there own. Tensions between the two become unbearable.

Marriages are never without stress, but where there is love, couples will find a way to address the stress in their situations before it becomes a problem leading to this cycle. Phase one as described by Walker is a loveless relationship. The presence of love in the relationship will provide for the courage to deal with the problem before it leads to phase two.

The acute-battering incident phase is the time when the batterer lashes out at his or her victim. There is none of the self-control that comes with love. Batterers always blame the victim for causing the blow up. They also claim that the stressful nature of their lives needs to end. This is the phase when tremendous physical injuries can and do occur.

When the acute attack is over, initial denial and disbelief that it has really happened usually follows. Both the batterers and their victims find ways of rationalizing the seriousness of such attacks. If there has been physical violence, the battered (more likely the woman) will often minimize her injuries. For example, a woman whose husband tried to choke her with a metal chain reported she was grateful she only had marks around her neck, rather than cuts from the chain breaking the skin. In minimizing the attack, a woman might say, "He only said that because he was angry. If he had been his normal self, he would not have said it."

Love always speaks the truth. Never cover up for your spouse. Speak the truth and it will open the door for your breakthrough. Many times the battered person chooses to protect the batterer in a pseudo-love. Real love speaks reality. The reality is the marriage is in trouble, and no covering up will solve the problem.

You hold the keys to your breakthrough. Call out for help; both you and the batterer need help.

The final phase, the kind-and-contrite loving behavior, is loaded with promises that further verbal assault and physical injuries will stop and never happen again. This phase generally keeps the relationship together and keeps both partners in denial. He/she enjoys being relieved of the inner stress, certain it will never happen again. The battered particularly enjoys the special attention the batterer gives. The couple that lives in a violent relationship becomes a symbiotic pair, each so dependent on the other that when one attempts to leave, both lives are drastically affected.

It is during phase three—when the loving kindness is most intense—that symbiotic bonding really takes hold. Both parties fool themselves into believing that together they can battle the world. The sense of over-dependence and over-reliance upon each other is obvious in each phase of the cycle. The bonding aspects of it, however, are laid down during phase three.

Ann Jones indicates, in *Next Time She'll Be Dead,* that while it is important to understand the cycle of abusive behavior on the part of men who batter women, battering must not be seen as isolated or random attacks. Jones puts responsibility where it rightfully belongs—on the batterers. It is vital to understand that battering is not a series of isolated blow-ups. It is a process of deliberate intimidation intended to coerce the victim to do the will of the victimizer. The batterer is not just losing his or her temper, not just suffering stress, and not just manifesting insecurity or spontaneous reaction. He is or she is usually provoked by something the victim does, or by his or her own inability to control anger.[8]

Therapists who work with batterers agree those are often-used excuses; yet, we all know aggravated, insecure, stressed-out people with meager interpersonal skills who lose their temper without becoming violent. Examples like this provide a convenient public excuse and deceive the battered person into giving the batterer another chance to be the so-called real, nonviolent man/woman within.

Christian therapists must join the abusers and advocates who want help by breaking the silence and calling abuse exactly what it is—sin.

Lenore Walker indicates, from her writing in *The Battered Woman,* that battered women believe the Bible says a woman is inferior and subordinate to her husband and she must accept a life of pain as her lot. This is so far from the truth. Both husband and wife are equal in the sight of God, and none should feel anything less in their marriage. However, if this is the belief of an abused wife, she might start, in her pain, to question that belief. It might be when her husband starts beating one of her children, or when she thinks she will be killed by his violence. It might be some influence from the outside, such as a friend's comment, an article on wife beating, or a sermon on the subject that prompts her. Others begin to question a biblical exegesis that suggests the use of power against them, from which they begin to see the Scriptures are more on their side than they thought possible.

All a batterer needs is for the people on the sidelines to join the silence of the battered spouse and remain quiet. Loving husbands and the church community *cannot* and *must not* remain quiet. Those of us who recognize the problem and have sought to understand it, using the various theoretical models, can vigorously fight against abuse.

Jan Horsfall suggests through her book, *The Presence of the Past,* the forming of "men consciousness-raising groups."[9] I do believe that loving husbands who are concerned about the adverse aspects of wife abuse should take it upon themselves to establish these life-giving groups. Just talking about the problems will not create awareness. Participants need to be emotionally involved. Since males have been poorly prepared for intimacy in general, developing a trusting environment in which they can display emotions will require hard work and determination. Husbands in such groups must eventually confront each other regarding such profound issues as power, sexuality, responsibility, and insecurity. Likewise, women would be well served to rise to the challenge and start care groups to help women deal with their problems in a better way than resorting to violence.

The church has a tremendous opportunity to help the batterer. More often than not, they first go to the pastor for help. Pastors have the opportunities, both directly and indirectly, to provide great support. The first place to begin might be, as Marie Fortune encourages in her book *Keeping the Faith,* "getting the abused out of danger."[10] Rita-Lou Clarke is in total agreement with Fortune. Kind people are needed who are willing to take in abuse victims and their children on a short-term basis, in the case of an emergency.

The homes should be used only as a last resort in case the woman is unable to get into a shelter or find other refuge. It is important to keep the location of those emergency homes secret to protect both the hosts and the battered. When wives leave, husbands often will hunt their wives, and when they find them they become violent with those attempting to help.

Lenore Walker, in her book *The Battered Woman,* lists common characteristics of battered women that the abuser, the church, and its leadership must know if as a corporate body we are going to provide help.

The battered woman:

1. Has low self-esteem

2. Believes all the myths about battering relationships

3. Is a traditionalist about the home

4. Strongly believes in family unity and the prescribed feminine sex-role stereotype

5. Accepts responsibility for the batterer's actions

6. Suffers from guilt yet denies the terror and anger she feels

7. Presents a passive face to the world but has strength enough to manipulate her environment to prevent further violence and possibly being killed

8. Has a severe stress reaction to psycho-physiological complaints

9. Uses sex as a way to establish intimacy

10. Believes no one will be able to help her resolve her
predicament

When counseling the battered, such characteristics as those listed above must be kept in mind. When informed helpers learn of a case of abuse, they can be prepared to offer leadership and counseling to batterers in their communities.

Loving husbands should help victims send a message to abusers who batter their spouses to stop and seek help. There are service agencies available to provide help. However, these groups are helpless without the cooperation of the abused and the abuser.

If you are presently an abusive spouse, it is my prayer that God will convict you of your actions and that you will seek help today. You can live a successful life and have a happy marriage with your love growing daily. The choice is yours. You are married for love, happiness, and peace. If these are not present in your relationship, there is help. If you are frustrated and tired of fights, there is help. If you are tired of the emotional putdowns and the physical and verbal abuse, there is help! If someone other than your spouse is offering you emotional support and is verbally affirming you, your marriage is in trouble. If you are being abused sexually, if you cannot find sexual fulfillment, and if you are living an unfulfilled life, there is help. Do not settle for a mediocre marriage when you are destined for marital success and excellence. If you are a Christian, go to an elder or a leader in your church, share your struggles, and request prayer. If your abuse includes physical abuse, please see a professional counselor or spiritual help. If your church does not have qualified help, many qualified therapists are available.

Happily married couples cannot afford to be silent bystanders because they are experiencing true love when others marriages are slowly dying. To be quiet is to play into the batterer's hands. As loving spouses, we are called upon to lead a crusade to restore agape love to husbands and wives, and to speak out against abuse. Our children are looking for a brighter tomorrow. If we remain silent, do not address the crime, and stem the disease, there will be more failed marriages. Will we be able to avoid blame?

The survival of humanity and the restoration of our personal humanity depend on our own answers to these questions.

## Discussion

1. Are women equal to men? If so, in what ways?

2. What was the purpose for Paul's injunction to women to be silent in church?

3. How does a person forgive someone who has abused him or her for years?

4. List the three phases of the abuse cycle.

5. If there are possibilities to build a marriage on the basis of nonviolence, what is the meaning of reconciliation?

6. How can we change the basic myth surrounding abuse?

7. Make a list of things you can do to help individuals whose marriages are on the rocks because of abuse.

8. Prayerfully ask God to help you reach out to hurting couples in love for you to be an example for them.

*Chapter 9*

# KEEPING LOVE ALIVE IN THE
# STAGES OF MARRIAGE

*Do not arouse or awaken love until it so desires.*
—SONG OF SOLOMON 2:7, NIV

MANY COUPLES ENTER marriage with fairytale expectations. Fairytales marriages are where the princess and her Prince Charming ride off into couplehood happily ever after. The message conveyed by the fairytale is love leads to marriage, and marriage leads to lasting happiness. Fairytales are just imagination. They are not real. Fairytale expectations suggest that all problems will disappear when Mr. or Mrs. Right comes along.

Other couples enter marriage expecting a perfect spouse. There is no perfect spouse. Each person entering marriage needs to understand they have married as flawed and imperfect a person as themselves. But with love, commitment, knowledge, patience, time, and God, they will be able to heal each other and make a wonderful marriage. Marriage fairytales are for young dreaming children.

As you contemplate marriage, whether you are married or not, you should be aware marriage has a "natural history," and it develops in identifiable stages. When couples know and understand the normal stages of marriage development, they will be better prepared to use the appropriate love at each stage of their relationship.

Each stage has its own problems and happiness. It is also important to note that the marital stages are not linear, but cyclical. As the marriage grows, there will be times of honeymoon, romance and fault finding etc, but because of a couples' commitment to grow and mature in their loving marriage, each cycle will build and strengthen the marriage love and intimacy. However, if a couple does not understand the stages of marriage, the lack of understanding will lead to frustration, disillusion, confusion, heartaches, stalemate, separation, and/or divorce. Safeguard your marriage by reading more about the stages of marriage.

When couples enter their marriage union with the knowledge and understanding that marriage goes through various stages, they would be better prepared to handle marital life situations when they do come. Further, learning about it while you are married will provide you with the knowledge to help you maximize and enjoy each stage together.

Going into anything without some knowledge or understanding of how it functions can lead to disaster. Getting into a car to drive without some knowledge, trainingt, and experience can be disastrous for the driver and other motorists on the road. Likewise, getting into marriage without proper knowledge and tools can be scary. Be wise and get knowledge and wisdom and it will provide success in your marriage.

I heard a story describing a couple's honeymoon. It sounded funny, but was loaded with problems.

A young couple got married and left for their honeymoon. When they got back, the bride immediately called her mother. The mom asked, "Well, how was the honeymoon?"

"Oh, mama," she replied, "The honeymoon was wonderful! So romantic…." Suddenly she began to cry. "But, mama, as soon as we returned, Andrew started using the most horrible language. He has been saying things I have never heard before! All those awful four-letter words! You have got to come get me and take me home…please mama!"

"Sarah, Sarah," her mother said, "Calm down! Tell me what could be so awful? What four-letter words has he been using?"

"Please do not make me tell you, mama," wept the daughter, "I am so embarrassed! They are just too awful! You have got to come get me and take me home….please mama!"

"Darling, baby, you must tell me what has happened to you to get you so upset….Tell your mother those horrible four-letter words!"

Still sobbing, the bride replied, "Oh, mama…words like dust, wash, iron, and cook…"

Many people are shocked into reality when they return home from their honeymoon, which should never be the case. This story tells us the couple is going to have some serious marital problems. To the new bride, it seemed her marital dreams were based upon fairytales.

A honeymoon is a time when newly married couples start their lives together on their own. It is a time to get to know each other intimately, bonding of their hearts into one. It is a time when couples begin to understand each other and put into practice skills learned in premarital counseling.

The honeymoon is a normal and pleasant part of most life experiences. There is a honeymoon-romantic stage in every relationship, including those with friends, a boss, a job, an adopted child, and marriage. Everything seems wonderful, and then the honeymoon is over—reality hits home. Frustrations or hurt feelings begin to mount. How we deal with reality is determined by the foundation that was laid.

Honeymoon is the period of time for the newly married couple, in their new environment, to understand each other, to evolve their own personal values, and to determine the course of direction of their marriage with commitment. It is the time when couples begin to build their corporate oneness. No longer living for "self," but now living for "us."

The honeymoon stage provides the couple with the time to experience and understand the negative and positive personality attributes of each other; of sexual values; and biological, physiological and psychological differences between a man and woman. It reveals the other's wants, desires, expectations, anticipations, ambitions in sex, and personal sexual values of the other. It reveals each other's true spirituality. It provides the opportunity to develop absolute care of the other, togetherness, privacy, sexual equality, sharing, and co-operation. Honeymoon provides the new couple with a learning environment where free, frank, and honest verbal and non-verbal communication will reveal oneself and provide the opportunity for adjustability, adaptability, and compatibility.

While couples are enjoying their honeymoon-romantic love, they should also use the time to initiate a strong base for their faith and spiritual development. Couples should understand the honeymoon period is more like a laboratory where two souls are welded together in an environment of trust, love, and understanding. It is like a classroom where both should begin to learn and understand each other in a more intimate way. Therefore, couples should take much time in their honeymoon stage to read, study, and pray together. The Word of God and the Holy Spirit are sure guarantees to help couples with the challenges and stresses that come in marriage.

For couples planning to getting married please note that perfect honeymoons do not just happen. They have to be carefully planned. The more you do your honeymoon homework, the more romantic, and the more fun, your honeymoon will be. Having given that little nugget, let us get back to the issue at hand.

Sociologist, Dr. Linda Waite, a top family scholar at the University of Chicago, and Maggie Gallagher, director of the marriage program at the Institute for American Values, discuss the enormous multidimensional benefits of being married. In their book, *The Case for Marriage*, they state, "Honeymoon sets the stage for a wonderful experience, that would extend your life span by up to eight years, improve your immune system, reduce the incidence of physical, mental, and substance abuse disorders, help you recover from illness and surgery more quickly, result in more satisfying and more frequent sexual relations, and increase your financial net worth."[1]

A good foundation provides a sure structure on which to build anything in life. Jesus tells us a story in Matthew 7:21–28 about the necessity of proper spiritual foundation. When a house is built on a foundation of rock, it will withstand the rain, wind, and storms of life. However, when a house is built on sand, it will not be able to withstand the same tests and trials as the house built on rock. The principles are the same for marriage.

Honeymoon provides the opportunity for couples to build a good foundation. If the foundation is laid on the Word of God, prayer, love, respect, and intimacy, then the Dr. Waite words are a sure guarantee. If the marriage foundation is properly laid, couples will be able to navigate the stages of marriage, use each stage as a building block of love and intimacy, and experience longevity of life and the wonderful benefits outlined above by Dr. Waite.

The honeymoon is not designed to last forever! The love and passion experienced in the honeymoon should extend toward one another and be used to build a solid foundation and avoid potholes along the way. A honeymoon launches the celebration of formal commitment and covenant you have made to God, family, and friends. When the honeymoon is over, your commitment to continue loving your spouse will be the main ingredient for keeping happiness and joy in your marriage.

Your love should motivate you to seek your spouse's best, no matter what the cost. Sometimes love will be an act of will in the midst of conflicting feelings. Generally speaking, married couples know love does not come easy. Marriage love takes a lot of hard work, and it will be the governing factor in each stage of marriage that will get you over the hump of life's trials and difficulties.

Your feelings, as mentioned before, will come and go. There will be days when you do not feel love for your spouse. You may feel angry, hurt, disgusted, disappointed, and exhausted. Yet, you are still called to love your wife or husband as you promised on the day you were married, in all circumstances, despite your feelings. That is the secret happy, gray-haired older couples understand. Love is the glue that binds a marriage and guarantees it will stand the test of time. The love factor in marriage will sometimes be steamy and sizzling, but there are other times when it will require a jumpstart. The jumpstart will be an act of love that is given without the aid of oxytocin, PEA, or any other chemical.

## LOVE BEYOND THE HONEYMOON

The first year of marriage is often a busy time with many transitions. Much of the time will be spent together involved in daily tasks—cleaning, cooking, shopping, driving, showering, and sleeping. The question here would be: do I use that as real quality time? It is important for newlyweds to continue to make time for dates and do the things they did together when they first began dating. They should continue to make getting away together a priority. They should try to schedule two weekends a year (at least) that they

THE LOVE FACTOR IN MARRIAGE

can take off together. That would be a time of refreshment for their relationship in sharing time together away from normal life.

Those vacations will provide exclusive time. If both spouses express care, appreciation, and love to each other, they may end up taking another honeymoon. They should not try to rush when it happens. They have to think and feel positively toward each other. Then when time and circumstance permits, they can choose together to have that period of "honeymoon time" with each other once again.

To quote Sharyn Wolf, in her book, *So You Want to Get Married:*

> The end of the honeymoon is not a wall; it is the next perimeter of human experience, filled with great promise. In order to get through that perimeter you need...the willingness to risk, a belief that something good will come from this, the faith that you are working toward something worth having, and plenty of energy. When you have the energy to want to throw each other out the window, you also have the energy to make your relationship work.[2]

As Christian couples, you must always remember you are not alone. God gave you the Holy Spirit to guide you in your new experience. Keep Him as your loving Guide and Partner in marriage, and He will give you the strength to persevere through the good and bad times as you build a lasting and pleasurable marriage. The Holy Spirit will help your love blossom, grow, and bring forth loving fruit in the marriage through nurture and care. For as your love grows your intimacy also will grow. Many marriages fail for lack of true intimacy.

Why does something that starts out feeling so good seem to go downhill once you take that step of commitment? How could lovers who become alive and swept up into powers beyond their control or reasoning seem so love starved? Those are questions many couples ask when conflicts and problems arise in their marriage and intimacy begins to change. Why does the love seem to go away? Well, one of the culprits is couples do not know about the stages of marriage and they tend to be stuck in one of the early stages rather than moving through them, growing in love. They begin to feel disillusioned and trapped in frustration and disappointment.

Many couples have given up on the marriage when the honeymoon is ended for lack of feeling loved. They claim they no longer love each other. Then they go on to start other relationships that end in divorce 75 percent of the time. Those couples make the wrong choices to end their marriage. Their love was wounded, not dead. Another spouse will not change the love problem, but rather a mental change would.

A euphoric feeling of love usually blinds couples in the first stage of marriage. Because of the euphoric feelings, many couples are stuck in stages two or three. Because they are stuck, hurt and damage occur. Around 50 percent of those married couples will decide to divorce; the other 50 percent either withdraw from one another and live in a politely superficial marriage, or they continue to find fault or blame and may abuse each other for decades. Most abuses in marriage tend to happen when couples get stuck at one stage for too long.

The stages in marriage take on new intensity. But with the commitment to love each other regardless of the challenges faced in each stage, the intensity can be used to build love rather than destroy love. There is much more at stake when we make a commitment to spend our lives together to love and be loved. What is done after the honeymoon stage is key; it will determine the quality and quantity of years a couple will have together.

Listed in the following sections are the stages of marriage. Understanding those stages will lead couples to build better and loving marriage relationships.

## Stage I: Romantic Love— "You Are Perfect"

This stage often feels so good you want it to last forever. In fact, couples wish it could last forever! Everything seems perfect at first. You feel energized, alive, and filled with new dreams. Your heart is filled with love, and you know your spouse loves you. When things appear that you do not like, it is denied or at least minimized. Couples tend to go above and beyond what is required or expected. You find many creative ways to express your love. Oh, and when you are apart, you keep thinking of your beloved. Everything feels right. Many people feel a sense of finally being at home or of being complete, feeling alive and connected. Really, what is happening here is there is a flood of chemicals flowing through the body. They are producing loving highs.

When a person falls in love, a peptide, PEA (phenoethalymine), is produced in the body. PEA increases energy, feelings of well-being, positive outlook, and diminishes pain. It increases sexual desire. It causes couples to stay up until 4 a.m. and go to work the next morning as if they had a full night's sleep. They can be so caught up in being with the other person that they miss a meal and do not really notice. If they usually tend to be anxious, PEA may help them feel calm. If they are usually depressed, they might see things more positively. They believe it is the other person that brings out the best in them and at last they have found the perfect one! To some extent, that may be true, but they would not know until the PEA decreases.

Couples who possess a strong commitment to the marriage covenant and to their relationship normally experience the greatest benefits of romance at all stages of marriage. A strong commitment is not difficult to maintain if the relationship is characterized by closeness, romantic love, and the love of God. We cannot divorce romantic love from God's love. God gives romantic love, and He must be an integral part in order for the romance to be balanced and whole.

Following the romantic phase, the marriage moves into a period of disappointment and disillusionment which is brought on by the normal stresses of marriage, unmet expectations, and the undeniable reality that one's partner has faults. In other words, the rose-colored glasses become clear. It is during this time commitment to marriage becomes a greater challenge as couples begin asking the question, "Is this all there is?" It is here love junkies begin experiencing doubts and growing couples know they have come to the end of the first stage and are now entering the faultfinding stage.

## STAGE II: FAULTFINDING—
## "YOU ARE FLAWED"

The faultfinding stage is sometime known as the "disillusion-ment phase" of marriage. Here couples are faced with the choice of proceeding down one of two paths. The first path involves a decision to avoid confronting the issues that have contributed to the sense of disappointment, faultfinding, and settling into a safe, but lonely, relationship devoid of any real intimacy. Couples who choose to travel that path do not experience the same level of benefit from their marriage and are more vulnerable to giving up when pressures arise.

The second, healthier path involves a willingness on the part of the couple to courageously and lovingly address their faults and inadequacies while making an effort to be more understand-ing and accepting. They make a conscious decision to view each other positively, and they seek God's guidance through His Word, prayer, and the living presence of the Holy Spirit—the Comforter. Couples who choose to walk down that path are in a much better position to experience the full benefits of marital bliss.

With the help of one's spouse and God, couples who own up to their relationship challenges and face them head on are those who maintain a shared commitment to love, and they value the covenant of marriage. Their commitment is based on the love of God in their hearts and the love for each other, knowing the real-ity of life's circumstances will change and so must the marriage, if it is to grow. Change is necessary for every living being; it is one of the most difficult things for people to accept. The sooner couples accept the challenges, change, and adjust to it, they will be able to enjoy life as God created it to be.

If you are married or thinking about getting married some day, give yourself the greatest advantage you can possibly have for making your marriage a success—begin a close and per-sonal relationship with God, and He will guide you through the difficult times. As a child of God, you are never alone in your relationship. You can hear the psalmist David say, "The Lord is my Shepherd, I shall not want....Yea though I walk through the valley of shadow of death I will fear no evil, for thou art

with me..." (Ps. 23:1, 4, KJV). That psalm should be an anchor
in your marriage. God is your Shepherd, and He will lead your
marriage to green pastures, as long as you stay committed to
Him and your spouse.

Maintaining a strong commitment, possessing the right attitude, and choosing to love someone who does not always act in a
loving way can be very difficult. But, through the power and love
of God, you can be equipped to meet those challenges and consequently experience the wonderful benefits of marriage!

The conflicts within the faultfinding stage are allowed by God
to help you and your spouse realize your potential as individuals
and as a couple! Couples need to see and accept conflict as an
opportunity to provide healing for personal and marital growth.

The faultfinding stage is God's invitation to the oneness growth
process. This stage allows couples to move beyond the chemical
rush of love. In the beginning of most marriages, many spouses
see the other spouse as the source of their good feelings, so they
blame the other spouse when they do not feel as good as they
want to. They fail to realize the change in marriage was simply
God's way to allow couples to practice loving actions, which
would lead to loving feelings. The change in the love chemical
rush gives couples the opportunity to control their feelings of
love. It gives them the power to turn on or off their love feelings.
They become the controller of love's feelings, rather than being
controlled by love feelings.

It is here some illusions begin to die and expectations are
diminished or shattered. The burden of unmet expectations by
yourself and your spouse are exposed. It sometimes feels as if love
is dying. Some couples might pretend that the disappointment,
frustration, and hurt are not really there or that they should not
be upset. They may try to explain things away or even attempt
to pray it away. It is called denial. Denial is not the answer. This
stage should be embraced as an open door to deeper connection,
intimacy, and a fulfilling relationship. Conflict and distress in the
faultfinding stage hold the key to mutual growth, healing, and
fulfilling your potential as individuals. It is the point where you
wake up, decide to become conscious and intentional in the mar-

riage, and begin a completely new chapter in cocreating the relationship of which you both have dreamed. It is in this stage that unconditional love is fully released.

In this second stage, you might start feeling anxious or disappointed. Things you once liked about your partner have become sources of frustration and hurt feelings. You may ask, "What has happened to him/her/us?" There is a sense of betrayal or loss. What have you really lost? PEA bliss. Couples become adversaries instead of partners. If couples allow themselves to become adversarial, they engage in blame, criticism, sarcasm, and putdowns. Then anger and resentment will build. Sometimes, it may feel as if you are walking on eggshells. Little things tend to easily turn into big things. The struggle is on.

Winning and being right becomes more important than working together and cocreating the loving, fulfilling relationship you both desire. Here,, Satan is working through the desires of the flesh to destroy and ruin your marriage. It is important to realize the devil wants couples to dwell on their negative feelings in order to immobilize the marriage. As the negative feelings mount, demonstrations of love, respect, and appreciation decline; it may even disappear with neglect. If enough distress builds, you may begin avoiding your spouse as much as you can. On the other hand, a spouse may turn to something else—work, children, a hobby, house chores, or, dare I say, ministry—as a way to attempt meeting his or her needs and to avoid the distress.

It is at this stage many ministers and laity begin to lose their marriages. Spiritualizing your problem will not cause it to disappear. Becoming more involved and dedicated in church activities, will not alleviate the problems.

Do not run away from your problem—face it and grow. It does not matter how many things you do in the name of religion, it will not fix your marriage. Instead, the more you get involved in ministry outside the home and neglect your family, the more you are separating yourself from the blessing of God. A couple's priority should be their marriage and family, then the ministry.

This stage is the breaking or bonding point for many couples. For some couples this stage can reach a level of desperation where they have tried everything they know, and it seems the only option is to get out—temporarily or permanently. It is at this stage you need to use God's unconditional love to weather the storm of faultfinding. When you call upon Him, His Spirit will come to your aid and give you divine insight as to what you can do to be a healing agent. He will give you the fruits of the Spirit to build your love in God and in your spouse.

Too many couples give in to hopelessness and despair at this stage. Often, well-meaning friends or family members encourage them to get rid of their spouses. Other couples try to just cope with it, resigning themselves to a workable living arrangement. Some stay together because of the kids because they are afraid people will judge them, or because of financial concerns. They end up living in the same house disconnected from one another. Other couples remain in their marriage because of ministry and status in the church community. God has enough love to heal your marriage so you do not have to stay for those laudable reasons.

Many call it the "faultfinding or disillusion stage" the unfolding of ones' true self. The focus at this stage is identifying each other's needs and asking God for His wisdom to help engage in caring behaviors that are specifically targeted to meet those needs. This is the launching pad for handling the faultfinding stage. What couples need to realize is even when they are noticing faults, it indicates their love connection with their spouse is still alive. Faultfinding provides the opportunity for spouses to cocreate each other through healing and personal growth. It means each spouse has a chance to help build each other in love through nurturing and caring. Couples must take time to learn how to communicate and negotiate constructively each other's faults in a loving way that will minimize hurts and pains. How these issues are dealt with will determine how quickly and smoothly the couple will move to the next marital stage.

## STAGE III: COOPERATION— "WE WILL DO IT TOGETHER"

In this stage, couples have grown to accommodate each other for who they are, and they are working to renew their relationship by fulfilling each other's needs. As they cooperate, a door opens to deepen their connection, build intimacy, and reinforce a more fulfilling relationship. Here they constantly look for new information and insights to nurture their marriage or relationship. They do things together to build the marriage. Each spouse takes time to learn and practice new ways of pleasing each other, but they start with personal changes that will enhance the marriage. Building this stage requires much help.

Where can couples go to get help with new information to help them build the marriage? First and foremost, they can go to the Word of God. God is the Creator of marriage and His Word has much to say. They can talk to godly married couples, couples with a good testimony that have been married for at least thirty years. They may want to talk with a Christian counselor or visit workshops that teach relationship skills.

This is the stage in which you not only recognize your relationship can be more than it is, but also you have the power to make real changes. It is also here that husbands, as the loving heads, choose to become conscious and intentional cocreators of the kind of relationship he and his wife dreamed of and that God intends.

While one or both may continue to feel anxious, confused, or afraid and may resist making some of the changes at this stage, the husband needs to take charge of the direction of the marriage, and with God's help, chart the course to joy, happiness, and peace. He needs to start intentionally learning how to become the right partner. By setting a good example his wife will be able to follow.

## STAGE IV: ACCEPTANCE—
## "HARMONIOUS LIVING"

The acceptance stage sounds like this, "Well, that is the way he or she is, I will have to learn how to live with him or her. I have tried all I know how; there is no changing him or her. I have resolved there is no hope. I am stuck. He is a good man, but he just will not take the garbage out. She is a good lady, but she does not like to vacuum, so I will."

In this stage, couples commit to becoming more intentional in their care and love for each other, instead of reacting to each other's differences. Couples hold, in their minds and hearts, the vision of the relationship they want, and they work each day to make their marriage reality.

At the acceptance stage, each partner switches from the consumer to creator. Each partner takes responsibility for their own problems and sheds the illusion that their spouse is the key to their happiness.

Jawanza Kunjufu says in his book *Restoring the Village Values and Commitment: Solutions for the Black Family*, "You and your mate realize that regardless of who you are with, there will be problems, so I might as well stay in the relationship and work them out."[3]

According to Less Parrott in his book *Relationship,* this acceptance "is the bridge to ultimate transformation and a love that can be enjoyed for a lifetime."[4]

## STAGE V: REAL LOVE—TRANSFORMATION "WE GROW TOGETHER"

This is the final stage. Couples begin to appreciate the benefits of love and patience which help them weather the trials of marriage. Couples have developed a deep respect and appreciation for one another as separate and unique individuals. The real-love stage is only possible for couples who are truly committed and are willing to do the hard work to gain the benefits of marriage.

Romance is the launching pad God uses to start the lovemaking process, which leads to real love. The road between romance and real love requires a lot of knuckling down and a conscious desire to build a great love life.

Many therapists believe people reach this stage at age fifty or sixty. Here, at the real-love stage, couples try to do all they can to make each other happy and avoid doing things that are displeasing to the other. Here, couples are living for each other's happiness.

The real-love stage is a stage of intimacy, joy, passion, happiness, and peace. Couples at this stage live out the vision of true partnership—unconditional love. Here each spouse sees the other spouse as his or her best friend. This is the stage of oneness and wholeness.

A major problem in marriage is that many couples want to experience real love overnight. Wake up and face reality, stop dreaming—that is not possible. Real love can only be attained through hard work, persistency, commitment, and reliance on the Word of God and the infilling of the Holy Spirit. If you need help in your marriage, get it! Do not settle for mediocrity or a plateau. Do not throw away your hard-earned investment in a love relationship or listen to naysayers.

Divorces and breakups of committed relationships do not need to happen. You can make the marriage relationship a gift for yourself, your spouse, and your children. What a legacy to leave them and your world! Cultivate the attitude, "We grow together!" At the real-love stage, couples learn to reflect on the ups, downs, bumps, and bruised egos along the journey then look forward to good times ahead. In this final stage, couples know what the fairytale neglected to mention: love is patience, persistence, and hard work.

Dr. Hendrix states in his book, *Keeping the Love You Find,* that "each stage arises out of the prior stage, but each new stage carries forward the achievement or failure of the preceding stage."[5] Therefore, when each stage is handled properly, it will lead to true love. If the stages are not handled properly, then couples will live in mediocre marriages or get divorced.

When we feed our relationships with tender loving care, it counteracts our tendency to blame problems on our spouse. It allows us the privilege to think of many reasons we should be grateful to our partners. Disagreements are still part of real love, but couples find ways to resolve them and maintain love. Rather than holding on to anger, they instead choose to forgive and trust. Armed with the presence of the Holy Spirit and unconditional love, couples easily learn to live the lessons of mature and lasting love, loving someone in spite of what he or she does wrong.

If couples make it through stage three or four, the final stage of their marriage is there to enjoy and pass on to their children and grandchildren. So, instead of focusing on the love that is missing, begin to see and appreciate the love that is present. Realize you are not settling for less, you are maximizing the love that is present in the hopes more will come as you nurture what you have today.

## Discussion

1. List the stages of marriage.

2. Do you have any honeymoon memories?

3. Is there a difference between real love and reality love? Discuss.

4. What role did PEA play in your love?

5. Is your marriage love growing or are you stuck at one stage?

6. If it is stuck, what plans do you have to move on?

7. How were you able to cross over from the romantic stage to the faultfinding stage?

8. If you are not married, how will this chapter prepare you for marriage?

9. How can you use unconditional love to restore romantic love?

## Chapter 10

# LOVE AND INTIMACY

*My lover is to me a cluster of henna blossoms from the vineyards of En Gedi.*

—SONG OF SOLOMON 1:14, NIV

NTIMACY, WHAT IS that? Well, Webster's defines *intimacy* as, "The state of being intimate." However, one of the simplest and most understandable ways to describe it is to break the word down as "in-to-me-see." The definition is what intimacy is really all about—allowing another person to see into us, sharing and revealing who we are with another person. Allowing ourselves to be totally vulnerable in intimacy is one of the most difficult tasks for many people. Why is it difficult for many people to truly share real intimacy? Sin is the cause.

Sin has destroyed intimacy. Satan caused Adam and Eve to break their divine relationship and intimacy with God in the Garden of Eden. Sin destroyed and removed the loving innocence in the marriage relationship that Adam and Eve experienced. Prior to the entrance of sin, Adam and Eve experienced pure agape love.

As a result of Adam and Eve's sin, they experienced guilt and shame. Guilt and shame were passed on to humanity. Today, there are many people inside and outside the Christian church that are carrying the wounds of guilt and shame, which limit their capacity to be truly intimate. We present our wounds and burdens to our intimate other, then we expect them to undo the damage created by deficient nurturing.

Whenever there is a wound in personal intimacy, it spills over into the church community. Matthew 24:12 tells us, "Because of the increase of wickedness, the love of most will grow cold." When love grows cold in a relationship, intimacy suffers. Loss of real intimacy is one of the first signs that love is wounded and

111

that the relationship needs an intimacy check up.

If you are not feeling as intimate toward your spouse as you know you ought to be, it is time for an intimacy checkup! Do not settle for mediocre intimacy. You were made to experience a rich and wonderful intimate relationship. Keep reading and you will find out how you can rebuild intimacy.

Fear is one of the biggest intimacy killers. It is one of the biggest culprits that causes many to be afraid of intimacy. Why is that so? When individuals experience abuse, hurt, and pain in their early relationships of life, caused by family members, parents, friends, churches, and communities, they develop fear. There are many communities that support abuse through lack of knowledge or by ignoring the effects of the pain and hurts of the victims. The victims are afraid to trust another person or system for fear of pain or hurt. Their bad experiences cause victims of abuse to build emotional walls around themselves for protection.

Many individuals cannot or will not open their hearts fully to a loving relationship. For them, being intimate means someone will get hurt! Therefore, they live in false intimate relationships.

While writing this book, I was counseling with a friend who had been wounded emotionally. During the counseling period she concurred that emotional pains and hurts prevented her from trusting others, becoming truly intimate with people, and, worse, being fully intimate with God. She felt that there can be no true encounter with God until emotional issues are resolved or her life was made whole. She believes that healing can only come when she admits her hurts and pains and gives them to God.

The good news is that, due to her desire to reestablish her intimacy with God, she opened herself and gave her hurts and pains to Jesus Christ her Lord and was miraculously made whole.

I would like to share that it was not done in one session of counseling. Some emotional pains and hurts can be handled in one therapeutic session, but some will take time. Her therapy took a few sessions, Thank God, she is whole today because of the healing power and presence of the Holy Spirit in her life.

How do you know those who are fearful of intimacy or if you are among those kind of people? Look at the following comments:

"I will never get married." "You cannot trust men or women." "All men or women are liars and cheats." "Women or men are just interested in breaking one's heart."

That type of comment reveals the inner character of hurting people, whose previous relationships equaled pain, discomfort, or disappointment. They are living with painful memories and negative emotions. Those emotions exist inside, and the individual is the only one with the ability to control or change them.

If they can accept that residing in them is the power of God to control and or change the negative emotions, then they will have the opportunity to find trust and witness a depth of affection only limited by faith in God and an open imagination.

Fear of intimacy prevents many people from using their God-given power of unconditional love to conquer their false intimacy. You need to identify the fear that is hindering your intimacy and seek help removing it. Then real intimacy will be restored.

There are five types of fear that hinder intimacy: merger, abandonment, exposure, attack, and destructive impulses. You have the power to pull down those strongholds. You can overcome all fear in your relationship by calling on the God of love to fill you with His love. John tells us, "There is no fear in love. But, perfect love drives out fear, because fear has to do with punishment. The one who fears is not made perfect in love" (1 John 4:18).

Love will create in you a renewed mind. A renewed mind will lead to positive behavior that will replace negative fears and restore a real intimacy.

The apostle Paul gave a prescription for the cure of fear, "Do not copy the behavior and customs of this world, but be a new and different person with a fresh newness in all you do and think. Then you will learn from your own experience how His ways will really satisfy you" (Rom. 12:2, TLB).

Our minds hold to a belief that restricts our ability to love or trust. The therapy comes with a renewed mind, as the apostle Paul wrote, "be transformed by the renewing of your mind. Then you will be able to test and approve what God's will is—his good, pleasing and perfect will" (Rom. 12:2).

You are not born with fear nor are you destined to have it for the rest of your life. When you know how to let it go, God will remove the invisible scars of your experiences. He places the church as a loving community to foster intimacy.

Today, many churches are having couples' classes to teach couples how to maximize their love relationships. God is also rising up many godly Christian therapists who are writing books to help Christian couples live more fulfilled intimate lives.

Many couples are still living in false intimacy for lack of knowledge. The Word of God declares, "My people are destroyed from lack of knowledge. Because you have rejected knowledge" (Hos. 4:6). There is no reason for you to remain ignorant. Many Christian books exist to help you overcome false intimacy. Make a choice to restore your intimacy today. Go to a Christian bookstore immediately, and find a book that can help. Decide today not to live in false intimacy anymore.

The body of Christ has the answer to help you live in fuller intimacy. God is restoring a fresh love in the church. Many denominational walls are crumbling. As a result, local churches are joining forces to pray and evangelize their communities. Why are they doing that? What is the motivation behind the change?

Many denominational priorities have changed, and they find common goals to reach the lost for the love of God. Jesus Christ the Bridegroom is getting ready to come for His bride—the church. As His return draws near, the love thermometer rises. As the love thermometer rises in the church, so do the marital love relationships in the church. Genuine Christians are known by the love they show, according to John 13:34–35. The love of God, fully operating in a church, will release the love in marriage that produces intimacy, which is full of self-disclosure, openness, willingness to risk, understanding, and being noticed. That is truly real intimacy.

Dr. Harry Schaumburg, in his book *False Intimacy*, said, "There are three types of intimacies, the perfect intimacy, the real intimacy, and false intimacy."[1] The perfect intimacy was a pre-Fall relationship experienced by Adam and Eve. They were naked and unashamed. According to Dr. Schaumburg, "They enjoyed sexuality and relationship with the purest and fullest pleasure without hesitation and self-doubt. They romped, played, and relaxed in the presence of God. Sex and marriage were at a pinnacle."

Real intimacy is the sexual and relational intimacy two spouses share within their committed, loving marriage. Real intimacy involves disappointment and fear because of an imperfect world. Fear is the biggest obstacle to intimacy. Learning to overcome fear in intimacy is the key to building true intimacy.

Yielding to God and being filled with the Spirit will provide the power to overcome fear.

False intimacy is a self-created illusion to help a person avoid the pains inherent in real intimacy. Many people choose false intimacy because they do not want to experience pain and hurt. Pain, hurt, guilt, and shame are results of sin. Nevertheless, the love of God and His Spirit will give you the power to be vulnerable and through your vulnerability build intimacy.

The Holy Spirit will give you the power to overcome the pain and hurt that comes with real intimacy. God wants marriage relationships to be loving, intimate relationships, but the devil has fooled many into sacrificing for a false intimacy. Do not succumb to that lie. Pursue real intimacy.

Dr. Douglas Rosenau was discussing intimacy in his book, *A Celebration of Sex*, when he said, "An intimate marriage + mature lovers = a fulfilling sex life."[2] Intimacy begins in a loving covenant partnership where care and communication play an integral part. Do not allow your marriage to be dominated by a false intimacy syndrome that is caused by fear of intimacy. Love is the key to real intimacy in marriage.

Intimacy is the light that dispels darkness. Intimacy is more than sex. Intimacy removes shame and guilt in relationships and builds a bond that is impenetrable.

You may have been married for years, but you may also be living in false intimacy. In a marriage covenant there are no secrets. Real intimacy involves a total openness to the body, emotions, and spirit.

Real biblical intimacy declares that in marriage, your body is a love gift to your spouse. It should not be used as a bargaining tool. "The wife's body does not belong to her alone but also to her husband. In the same way, the husband's body does not belong to him alone but also to his wife. Do not deprive each other except by mutual consent and for a time, so that you may devote yourselves to prayer. Then come together again so that Satan will not tempt you because of your lack of self-control" (1 Cor. 7:4–5). Pray and ask God for guidance to help you lovingly give of yourselves to each other by choice and not only by feelings.

Spouses must take time to affirm each other and build their partner's emotional love. The emotional bond between a husband and wife begins with what most of us call "falling in love." What causes us to be attracted to a particular person? Dr. Terry Wier says, in *Holy Sex:*

> The leading theory holds that, through our experiences during childhood and early adolescence, each of us develops a list of attributes for the opposite sex that we consider ideal. This list is called a *lovemap.* Such list making is mostly subconscious, but it incorporates all our experiences with the opposite sex (both good and bad). Including our opposite-sex parent, our school friends, people we see on TV or in movies, and so forth. Our lovemap may specify physical features, personality traits, or even status symbols, such as wealth or popularity.[3]

Generally, men seem to be attracted to a woman's physical appearance. Whereas women seem to be attracted to men who are slightly taller than they are and who are financially secure. "Mr. and Mrs. Right" are usually attracted to each other by some magnetic force. It is "love at first sight" especially if each matches the other's lovemap.

Medical research indicates pheromones also play a role in romantic attraction. Having parents with very different immune system proteins is believed to give children the advantage of a much stronger immune system. So it is true after all, that "the right chemistry" can be an important part of romantic attraction.

Take time to satisfy your spouse's number one emotional need. According to Dr. Harley, in his book *Fall In Love, Stay In love,* "The priority of emotional needs differs in marriage between husbands and wives."[4] In his findings, "A husband's emotional needs are best met through terrific sexual experiences, and wives emotional needs are met through affection." Find out what your spouse's number one emotional need is and take time to nurture each other accordingly.

Finally, take time to build each other up spiritually. Spend time in personal and couples' worship. Arrange time to read and study the Word of God and pray together. Join a couple's class in your church where you can discuss and share the Word of God as it relates to marriage.

God has designed husbands and wives to bond in intimacy in three ways: through their bodies, emotions, and spirits. However, before we can master our intimacy for each other, we must first demonstrate our love and intimacy with God. "Love the Lord your God with all your heart and with all your soul and with all your mind and with all your strength" (Mark 12:30).

If you are having problems with intimacy in your marriage and your love is cold, let me encourage you to restore your love for God first. Repent of your sins, confess that you cannot love without Christ, and invite Him to come into your heart. He will come in and flood your heart with His love.

Becoming one with Christ will overflow into your marriage. Jesus can and will change you, if you wholeheartedly seek Him. True intimacy with Jesus Christ will impact your intimacy in your marriage. When God's intimacy is alive in your life, your spouse will see the glory of God in you and will want to draw closer to you and God.

## DISCUSSION

1. Do you have a definition of intimacy?

2. Discuss what "in-to-me-see" means.

3. Are there any fears that are inhibiting your intimacy?

4. What can you do to nurture your intimacy?

5. What is a lovemap?

# Chapter 11

# LOVE AND SEX

*Strengthen me with raisins, refresh me with apples, for I am faint with love.*

—SONG OF SOLOMON 2:5, NIV

IT IS AMAZING how in a few decades our society has become saturated with all kinds of sexual messages and a faulty view of love. One cannot watch a television show without a scene showing someone participating in some sort of sexual activity. It is difficult to buy something that is not being sold with sexual messages. No one is safe from those messages. However, the last place to discuss love and sex is the church.

Sex is a holy gift God designed for marital union according to Genesis 2:24, "For this reason a man will leave his father and mother and be united to his wife, and they will become one flesh." God designed sex for pleasure, procreation, and bonding of two in marriage. The Christian community believes sex is holy and scared, but the church fails to teach, inform, or facilitate any discussion on those issues as if doing so would be blasphemy. To the contrary, the Bible teaches much on love and sex. Lack of teaching on sex and love has led our culture to pervert God's gift to humanity. I thank God that the church is finally rising to the challenge.

Today, you can go into many Christian bookstores and find authors and counselors writing about sex and love. Thank God! The church is mandated to teach the whole book, which includes the story of love and sex. For too long we have left it up to the secular, humanistic school systems and government to teach morality of sex and love. Thank God, the church is finally heeding the warning, "My people are destroyed from lack of knowledge. Because you have rejected knowledge, I also reject you as my priests; because you have ignored the law of your God I also will ignore your children" (Hos. 4:6). The church seemed to refuse to address those subjects because they were once considered private and personal. However, our culture and media have made those issues public and corporate forcing the church to address them.

## SEX AND THE CHURCH'S VIEW

One of the problems surrounding sex and love in our culture and the church is combining them together as one and the same. Sex and love are two separate issues. However, they are designed to work together for the benefit of marriage. Another problem is that for a long time the church considered sex a necessary evil that breeds greater conflict in human sexuality. The voices of many church fathers have not advanced a positive message for sex.

Eric Fuchs said, in *Sexual Desire and Love,* that Augustine allowed that sex is good, but passion and desire are sin. "For he who is intemperate in marriage, what is he but the adulterer of his own wife."[1]

Mary Ann Mayo, in *A Christian Guide to Sexual Counseling*, says Thomas Aquinas thought as long as sex was not enjoyable "marriage was acceptable for those unable to accept the requirement of monastic existence."[2]

And Tim Stafford, in *Sexual Chaos,* adds that Martin Luther presented sex as a necessary evil when he said, "Intercourse is never without sin, but God excuses it by his grace because the estate of marriage is his work."[3]

As a result of such teachings, today there are many Christians who are confused by the false messages they receive about their sexuality. Their theology and practices are not in line with true biblical understanding. They are confused because many churches and denominations do not have a theological stance on sex. The only education many church members receive about sex is from their school, peers, folk stories, or the media. It is no wonder there is such a problem with sex abuse in our society.

Sex was intended to reveal the mystery of God that is embodied in Him. Sexual intercourse is designed by God to be the force that solidifies the one-flesh mystery between man and woman in marriage. Sexual law begins at the first sexual encounter. It

119

is believed by many counselors that sexual union joins a couple together more deeply and completely than by parental bonds.

The apostle Paul sheds more light on the bond when he says; "What? Know ye not that he which is joined to an harlot is one body? for two, saith he, shall be one flesh" (1 Cor. 6:16, KJV). Again he said, "For this cause shall a man leave his father and mother, and shall be joined unto his wife, and they two shall be one flesh" (Eph. 5:31, KJV). These scriptures reveal the magnitude of the sexual bond that is established between a man and a woman. The above texts do not limit the bonding that results from sexual intercourse to marriage only. Sexual laws apply to all sexual activities within or outside of marriage, whether the sexual activity was done by force, cohesion, seduction, drugs induced, or mutual consent. The sexual law is applied in all sexual activities. Sexual law produces the bliss, ecstasy, and rewards it is intended to produce when it is between a husband and wife. When it is done contrary to God's law it produces guilt, shame, regrets, emotional scars, and disease.

## SEX AFFECTS THE WHOLE MAN

Dr. Terry Wier wrote, in his book *Holy Sex,* much of what I will be discussing in this chapter. The physical act of sexual intercourse ultimately affects us in three areas producing spiritual, emotional, and physiological consequences. Therefore, all sexual relationships prior to marriage must be dealt with and resolved before individuals are joined in holy matrimony.

There are many reports which tell us unresolved sexual issues will not go away on their own, but they must be addressed in their totality before healing and wholeness can be restored. To help us understand a little better, Dr. Wier reports, "When you exchange bodily fluids with another person (even when kissing on the lips) you are also exchanging blood cells, viruses, bacteria, and perhaps unknown infectious agents yet to be uncovered." He adds, "Most people do not realize this fact. When you have sex with someone, with regard to STDs (Sexual Transmitted Diseases), you are having sex with every sex partner they have ever had, every sex partner any of their sex partners have ever had, and so forth. Researchers have calculated some averages on this. For example, if an individual has had just six sexual partners in their lifetime, and each of them had just six partners, then you have been exposed to the STDs of not just six partners, but of sixty-three people. For nine sexual partners, you would have been exposed to the STDs of five hundred eleven people, and so on. The numbers grow much faster than simple multiplication."[4]

Dr. Wier further adds:

> When a husband's seminal fluid is first introduced into his wife's reproductive tract, it initiates a series of important changes in her immune system. Seminal fluid contains compounds that temporarily suppress her immune system, which soon learns to recognize and accept his sperm instead of mistaking them for infectious bacteria. This is important because sperm can live in the female reproductive system for up to five days. This means that if a couple is having intercourse once or twice a week on average, the wife will be carrying living cells from her husband in her body almost continuously for the rest of their married life. If this adaptive process fails, the wife becomes allergic to her husband's sperm. This can cause her great discomfort, and she will be unable to conceive by him.

It is amazing what science is revealing about the wonderful gift of sex. Each new finding is supporting God's rule for sex in monogamous husband and wife marriage.

Regular exposure to her husband's sperm for at least a year in advance of her first pregnancy protects a woman from eclampsia. According to Symptom Solution Tracker, eclampsia is, "preceded by a condition called pre-eclampsia which is characterized by a rapid rise in blood pressure, swelling (mostly in hands, feet, and face), headaches, visual disturbances, and rapid weight gain. Seizures, irritability, a rapid pulse, high fever, and increasing blood pressure characterize eclampsia. It may lead to a loss of consciousness, or coma. These symptoms usually occur in the last trimester."[5]

However, in the case of a woman who becomes pregnant through a brief affair with a man other than her husband, she is at greater risk for eclampsia because her body has adapted to her husband's genes but not to those of the other man. There is always a consequence when God's sexual law is broken.

There are other slow viruses that affect one's body when God's sexual law is broken. *Mononucleosis,* or "Mono" as it is commonly known, is "the kissing disease." The disease is considered by many North Americans to be a normal and unavoidable adolescent rite of passage. What many fail to understand is the disease has life-threatening complications when a person is first infected. The virus that causes it, *Epstein-Barr,* is now known to remain in the white blood cells for life and can cause lymphoma as a person grows older.

"When you exchange bodily fluids with another person (even when kissing on the lips) you are also exchanging blood cells, viruses, bacteria, and perhaps unknown infectious agents yet to be uncovered. But most people do not realize that fact." Expressing love and sex in the marriage union is the only way to protect oneself from breaking the sexual law. Those planning on getting married should refrain from kissing anyone on the lips other than your spouse-to-be.

One of the problems with most westerners is we are not socialized to think that way about kissing. Dr. Wier said, "When your romance reaches a point where you start kissing each other on the lips, then you have already made a serious commitment, whether you know it or not. By kissing someone on the lips, you are really saying: 'Babe, whatever you have got—herpes, mono, slow viruses—I do not care. I want it, and I am willing to bear the consequences for the rest of my life just for the pleasure of kissing you!' That is one serious commitment!" Research tells us 90 percent of sex is in the mind and the other 10 percent is the physical activity. The mind is referring not only to the mental function but also the physical function.

## THE CHEMISTRY OF SEX

Sex is not just a great feeling of ecstasy. Medical science has proven traditional cultures to be quite wise in their reinforcement of virginity and marital fidelity. Medical research tells us the sex drive is a very powerful force that originates in the body, yet its influence extends into the mind.

To begin with, we must understand that the initial force of

sexual desire is released through chemicals in our bodies. The level of *testosterone*, a hormone, in the bloodstream (in both men and women) determines how much sexual interest and desire we feel at any given moment.

If testosterone is "the lust hormone," then oxytocin is "the bonding hormone." Oxytocin is found in all animal species and is released whenever an emotional bond needs to be formed. In humans, oxytocin has been found to produce feelings of emotional intimacy and a desire for affectionate touch.

In *Holy Sex*, Dr. Wier reveals that medical research tells us both testosterone and oxytocin occur in both sexes, but as you might expect men have a much greater flow of testosterone and women have a much greater flow of oxytocin. In both men and women, oxytocin is released whenever someone, such as a friend or relative, touches you affectionately. Women also experience a great peak of oxytocin as they are giving birth. They experience additional flows of oxytocin each time they nurse their child, and so does the nursing infant. It seems to strengthen the mother-child bond. Both men and women experience a release of oxytocin after having an orgasm, but its effect is greater in women. That may very well explain the desire to cuddle and be close after sexual intercourse, which typically is stronger in women than men. Women also experience highs and lows of oxytocin during the menstrual cycle, which may explain their seemingly mysterious shifts from wanting frequent cuddling to not wanting to be touched. The mystery is revealed. guys. Our wives are driven by the power of oxytocin. Do not be confused with her mood changes; work to give her what she needs in love.

As a couple spends more time together, even in a casual dating relationship, they inevitably begin to touch more frequently—holding hands, kissing, and hugging. As they do those things, they are causing their bodies to release more and more oxytocin, which produces an emotional high and strengthens their emotional bond. That seems to cause a couple to become addicted to each other's touch. If they cease to touch for a period of time, because of travel or just being too busy, both will experience withdrawal symptoms, including depression, lovesickness, and a longing to touch each other again. The longer they go without touching, the weaker their bond grows.

That explains the problem many adulterers and adulteresses have after an affair. Affairs break the sexual law of God and release oxytocin, which creates a bond with the adulterous affair. That could also explain the reason for the behavior change in Sarah toward her mistress after Hagar slept with Abraham. "And Sarai said unto Abram, Behold now, the LORD hath restrained me from bearing: I pray thee, go in unto my maid; it may be that I may obtain children by her. And Abram hearkened to the voice of Sarai" (Gen. 16:2, KJV). Prior to her sexual relationship Hagar honored and respected Sarah and Abraham. But after she slept with Abraham and found out she was pregnant, the Bible said, "And Sarai said unto Abram, My wrong be upon thee: I have given my maid into thy bosom; and when she saw that she had conceived, I was despised in her eyes: the LORD judge between me and thee" (Gen. 16:5, KJV).

Hagar thought by sleeping with Abraham she became a lover, but it did not take long for her to be rejected by the true wife, Sarah. Sexual intercourse creates a bonding that causes individuals to feel ownership of the person's body they share. Hagar quickly learned that was not the case. As expected, researchers have now confirmed those suspicious parallels between addicts and lovers.

Besides the elevated levels of oxytocin already mentioned, PEA has been found at high levels in a lover's brain. It is believed that PEA acts as a natural amphetamine, a natural version of "speed."

There are other chemicals such as endorphins and encephalin that are also found in a lover's brain that act as natural opiates, relieving pain and giving a sense of well-being. When God designed us, I believe He did so to have us "addicted" to our mates. No wonder falling in love involves such powerful and overwhelming feelings! Your brain is getting itself "high" when your lover is around.

Many researchers believe the drug produces chemical changes in the brain that are similar to those experienced in a state of *limerence* (a term chosen to avoid the confusion surrounding "love," roughly equated with "being in love"). Essentially, PEA hijacks the chemistry of love, and the couple "falls in love" with the drug. That explains why many people are love junkies. They function on PEA highs that they gain through having multiple partners, rather than learning how to rekindle and use PEA with one spouse.

A much stronger degree of bonding occurs when a couple first has sex. A careful observation would reveal God designed us, and all animal life, to respond to and learn from pain and pleasure. All animals seek to avoid experiences that have been painful and seek to repeat experiences that have been pleasurable. In God's design, pleasurable things are good and painful things are bad.

When you discover your mate is the source of the greatest pleasure you have ever known, you will naturally want to keep him or her around as long as possible and keep doing whatever it was that felt so good! Not only does sexual pleasure bond you to your mate, but research has also shown that the pleasure you both experience actually prolongs and improves the quality of your lives.

In animal species that mate for life, the first act of intercourse between a courting pair causes a surge of hormones in their brains that imprints the sight and smell of their mate so they will remain faithful to each other. Another study has found, as the marriage relationship develops, spouses will often subconsciously agree which of them should do which task without any conscious discussion.

Sex not only has physical consequences, but spiritual consequences as well. There are three areas in which couples can be affected negatively: spiritual adultery, spiritual defilement, and demonic seduction.

Spiritual adultery takes place in the heart as Jesus declared, "But I tell you that anyone who looks at a woman lustfully has already committed adultery with her in his heart" (Matt. 5:28). Spiritual adultery precedes physical adultery. One may say committing adultery in the heart is not the same as the physical act, but it is still wrong because it is a betrayal of the mutual trust, honesty, confidentiality, and emotional intimacy between a husband and wife.

Spiritual adultery seems to be a particular danger for Christians, since we have so many opportunities for developing spiritual and emotional intimacy with others through praying together, counseling, or just sharing heart-to-heart. The situation requiring the greatest caution is obviously a man and woman working closely together or spending time alone together, while at least one is married to someone else. To avoid spiritual adultery, be sure to share all your thoughts and activities with your spouse for accountability and the security of your marital relationship.

The next spiritual problem is defilement. It occurs when one is affected by another person's sinful condition through spiritual contact with them. That is another rarely recognized way in which spiritual forces can directly influence our sexual feelings. Dr. Wier says, "When we accept that the human spirit is just as real as the body or mind, then it seems quite reasonable that our spirits could also be influenced by contact with another's spirit."

Would you agree there have been times when you met someone for the first time and felt uneasy about them in a way you could not quite put into words? You feel dirty and defiled by those people because your spirit has contacted theirs in some way. The greater our spiritual contact with another person, the greater our risk of spiritual defilement by them.

Sex is not just a physical act between two people; it is union. Within a sexual act, one's blood stream mingles with that of their sex partner. They are making themselves susceptible to any blood-borne diseases the other may have. If a person contracts a disease through an act of adultery, then your body can suffer for it with pain, sores, infertility, internal damage as various organs are eaten away, and perhaps even a considerably shortened life span.

Marital sex sets in motion the sexual laws of God and when it is upheld, the marriage grows healthy and happy. When it is violated, it produces significant problems in marital relationships.

Dr. Wier said, "The law of sexual union is a natural law comparable to the law of gravity. You can choose to break a moral law, but you cannot break a natural law. Natural laws determine the consequences of our physical actions." Based upon that view, sexual activities outside of marriage in any form is an attack on the sexual law of God and the consequences are sure.

## SEXUAL ROLES

When sexual intercourse takes place according to biblical standard, the law will produce its natural benefits and fulfill God's divine purpose. If it is done in violation of the sexual law, there will be devastating effects.

For women particularly, sexuality is another area that cultural inequities have infiltrated and undermined. Much of the sexual language and practices in our culture are demeaning to women. Sex has become an expression of conquest and control over, even hostility and violence toward, women rather than the expression of intimacy and connection.

The culturally imposed sex roles and sexual stereotypes with respect to gender are particularly devastating in the sexual arena. The sexual repression of men and women take quite different paths. Women in our society are cut off from enjoying the *physical* pleasure of sex; men are cut off from enjoying the *emotional* pleasure of sex. Women supposedly "give" their sexual favors; men "take" their pleasure. According to Dr. Wier, "Women are in essence cut off from sex, men from sexuality."

We have all heard the stereotypes: men only want sex, women only want love (affection); men enjoy sex, women do not. Furthermore, men should want only sex, while women should only want love. Boys are raised to view sex as a conquest; girls see it as something they do to get love.

A learned emotional ignorance makes it difficult for some men to experience sex as a vehicle for love or an expression of feeling and need. Men are generally socialized not to experience their feelings and emotions fully.

Women, on the other hand, have been denied orgasmic pleasure by the insistence they do not have orgasms or should not enjoy them. Physiologically, women are multiorgasmic, but women who openly express (or actively seek) their sexual pleasure are often degraded. Despite many books and the media's promotion of the sexually assertive woman and the fact many men say they wish their partners were more aggressive in bed, most women who take that approach are looked upon very negatively in marriage.

Couples should always seek to engage in sexual activity by mutual consent. The apostle Paul said:

> The husband should fulfill his marital duty to his wife, and likewise the wife to her husband. The wife's body does not belong to her alone but also to her husband. In the same way, the husband's body does not belong to him alone but also to his wife. Do not deprive each other except by mutual consent and for a time, so that you may devote yourselves to prayer. Then come together again so that Satan will not tempt you because of your lack of self-control.
> —1 CORINTHIANS 7:3–5

Couples must learn to say no to sex that feels like conquest or submission, that expresses hostility or anger, or is manipulative. Sex in a Christian marriage transforms the ordinary, reaching far beyond the mere meeting of two bodies and the release of tension to an ecstasy that testifies to God's love and grace.

For too long the church has been silent on the issues of love and sex. Today, the church is forced to deal with the sexually perverted culture. The western world's sexual revolution started in the Seventies. Earlier, the Sixties generation rebelled against commitment to institutions and corporate systems to establish individual rights. As a result of the individual rights, individuals began to express their love and sexuality freely as they made choices without corporate moral compass. That was called the free love and sex revolution. But it was not a sexual revolution, it was perversion of love and sex. Free love and sex led to some of the worse sexually transmitted diseases such as herpes, HIV, and AIDS.

According to Dr. Hendrix:

> "The true sexual revolution is, the revolution for sexual justice between the sexes, and for legitimizing sexual pleasure for women and emotional expression for men." He further says, "Since our attitudes toward sex are sociological rather than biological, they can be transcended. We need to recapture our sexuality in the same way as we break down the barriers of gender roles and stereotypes."[6]

To participate in the real sexual revolution in marriage, husbands and wives need to create a new sexual identity by *how they decide to act*. A relationship in which a man cannot be tender and a woman cannot be aggressive is a relationship that is in trouble and is a limited partnership. The marital goal is to be whole partners in whole partnerships. But the damage from cultural stereotypes has prevented many couples from fulfilling God's design.

According to Dr. Hendrix, "Transcending cultural stereotypes to experience our whole selves moves us toward androgyny." He believes human beings are inherently androgynous creatures, embodying both male and female energy, but the split in our culture is deep, and parts of ourselves are undernourished."

## Sexual Wholeness in Marriage

The word *androgyny* does not mean asexual, bisexual, or hermaphroditic, and certainly not unmasculine or unfeminine. Dr. Hendrix say that androgyny is our natural state of one sexual being. It refers to an *inner* balance and wholeness that allows us to be strong or gentle, logical or emotional, as required. Dr. Hendrix's definition of an androgynous person is "a man secure enough in his masculinity to permit the feminine aspects of his personality to emerge, or a woman secure enough in her femininity to permit the masculine aspects of her personality to blossom." A woman who identifies with the feminine and can access her masculine feelings is very powerful. Likewise, there is something extremely appealing about a masculine yet gentle man. Because many couples were not socialized to access their full resources, they tend to feel uncomfortable if they have to go outside the box to develop themselves. The box that couples need to govern their sex lives is God's Word. God has designed us as sexual beings so we can share our love with each other without fear, guilt, or any inhibitions.

Remember, God's the one who made us. If you go to Him in prayer and ask Him to help you be a gentler husband or a more assertive wife, He will help you. His words tell us "ask and it will be given to you; seek and you will find; knock and the door will be opened to you. For everyone who asks receives; he who seeks finds; and to him who knocks, the door will be opened" (Luke 11:9–10).

As you seek to master your God-given sexuality, what can you do to discover and develop your own innate sexuality and to increase the potential for sexual intimacy? You should become aware of your sexual history. Where you have failed, confess, repent, and ask for God's forgiveness. You must become conscious of the impact of sexual myths and stereotypes on your theology, behavior, and feelings, and then refuse to behave in accordance with those stereotypes and follow wholesome biblical standards.

For husbands, that might mean expressing the need for tenderness and being open to the *emotional* pleasure of sex. For women, it might mean expressing the need for sexual gratification and being open to the *physical* pleasure of sex. God wires your emotions to react freely to each other sexually, so do not be inhibited or bashful.

It means reversing roles and trying what is unfamiliar or uncomfortable for you such as being aggressive as a woman or perhaps allowing yourself to be passive, to receive, as a male. It certainly means having a sense of humor and playfulness, not taking it all so seriously. Imagination helps, too. It means *allowing* pleasure, including the pleasure of expanding into the other's awareness.

And it means dialogue. Communicate with your spouse just as nature intended. Many couples feel ashamed or uncomfortable discussing their feelings and desires; whereas, some other couples feel that if their spouses really love them, they would know what their emotional needs and desires were. No one can truly know what you are thinking or feeling without communication. So do not take for granted that your spouse knows what you need. And do not fall into the "if my spouse really loves me, he or she would know my sexual needs" trap. Therefore, the only way your feelings or desires can be known will be through communication. Communication is the gate to lead you into real and fulfilled love.

Real love might also be called "reality love." It is not based on the illusion of romance or the fantasy our partners will sense with our every wish and desire. Unlike romantic love, which centers on romantic yearnings, reality love is based on awareness, respect, communication, and commitment. Reality love is based on awareness and information about ourselves and our spouses, the healing purpose of our relationships, respect for our partners' needs and desires, and commitment to healing our partners through unconditional giving. So, help your spouse fully satisfy your God-given sexual needs and desires by talking—talking *and* listening!

Couples must talk about sex—exactly what they want, what they like, and do not like. Dialogue serves a dual purpose; it expresses your needs and desires, and it allows and requires you to consider the needs and desires of the other. By the way, let me remind you that sexual talk is itself erotic and breeds intimacy.

Couples need to maintain a healthy love and sex life in marriage if they are going to be able to weather the trials and difficulties of life. God gives those gifts to provide a way to keep the oneness in marriage that will keep happiness and peace amidst growth pains in marriage.

Keep love and sex alive in your marriage by always communicating your thoughts, desires, and feelings, because love and sex provide nourishment to the whole man—body, soul, and spirit. The physical act of sexual intercourse experienced in love will influence three areas, producing spiritual, emotional, and physiological consequences. Make sure it influences your marriage in positive ways. If it does not, do not be satisfied with mediocrity. Seek spiritual or professional help in order for you to be restored to whole health.

## DISCUSSION

1. What was your view of sex before you read this chapter?

2. What are the major points you have learned from this book?

3. Did any church fathers or mothers influence your view of sex?

4. Can you explain how God's law of sex works?

5. What do you think God had in mind for sexual law?

6. How important is sex in marriage?

7. What can you do to improve your views on sex?

8. If you are married, commit to improve your communication about sex.

*Chapter 12*

## LOVE'S REWARDS

*Above all, love each other deeply, because love covers over a multitude of sins.*

—1 Peter 4:8

MANY WONDERFUL GIFTS, benefits, and blessings have been passed on from generation to generation. The greatest gift mothers and fathers can give their children is the understanding of a healthy love life expressed through each child's love language. According to Dr. Gary Chapman, in his book, *The Five Love Languages,* "love language is that emotional vehicle through which one feels and experiences love."[1] When husbands and wives find each other's love language and communicate in them around their children, they will be establishing a wonderful foundation for their children's lives.

Dr. Chapman further states:

> Children who feel loved by their parents and peers will develop a primary emotional love language based on their unique psychological makeup and the way their parents and other significant persons expressed love to them. Children who do not feel loved by their parents and peers will also develop a primary love language.

Dr. Chapman modified those descriptions by saying, "Poor programming does not mean they cannot become good communicators. But it does mean they will have to work at it more diligently than those who had a more positive model."

George Barna, president of the Barna Research Group, noted on his Web site the impact widespread divorce has left on young people:

One of the most striking findings in our recent survey among teenagers is that when we asked them to name their top goals for the future, one of the highest rated was to get married and have the same spouse for life. That is a remarkable goal—one that reflects their own exposure to, and rejection of, a family that has to survive divorce, for whatever reasons. Since millions of those teens have never had a healthy marriage modeled for them, we can only pray that they will have the strength of character and the support systems available to make their goal a reality.[2]

Many children do not have a realistic view of marriage. They have flawed models around them and they are waiting for someone to show them the way.

Different family traits determine the emotional growth of children. However, a husband's love for his wife is one of the greatest ingredients necessary for emotional health and maturity. When husbands fulfill the command to love their wives, they are modeling an attitude and behavior that will provide a solid foundation for their children's future happiness. Raising emotionally stable children is only possible in a loving environment. Adults who lived in homes where there were loving relationships between the parents, will more likely provide a loving environment for their children.

Society expects children to demonstrate love to their mothers and fathers—usually through obedience. However, I have observed that children find it easier to love and obey their parents when they see them demonstrate love to each other. A careful look at the command given to husbands to love their wives and for wives to submit to their husbands reveals that children are to obey their parents in the Lord, subsequent to the parents loving and submitting to each other. In my opinion, the greatest gift a husband will ever give to his children is the love he expresses to their mother.

One of the biggest problems in our society today is most homes are starving for love. Because some women are changeable and moody, men sometimes get confused and find it difficult to display love to their wives. When they realize it is happening, husbands must put a concentrated effort into their marriage.

Men generally function from a logical point of view; whereas, women function from an emotional point of view. A husband may give his wife a rose today to demonstrate his love to her, but if he tries the same thing the following day it may not be accepted. The husband may not understand why she is not receptive the second time. It is important to note God did not command husbands to understand their wives, but He did command husbands to love them. When husbands shower their wives with love, they will, with the help of God, be able to meet their every need and build a healthier environment for their children. A properly loved wife and mother is a happy person, which in turn produces a happy and loving home in which to rear children.

Today, because of love-starved homes, many of our children are turning to drugs, gangs, sex, violence, videos, and suicide as their answer. The public school systems have failed our children because the government has removed God from education. Many of our churches are stuck in their traditional mold, and their youth ministries somewhere at the bottom of their priority list. Society is no longer child friendly. The movie and video industries have robbed our children of their innocence; there is nothing sacred anymore. Homes are no longer a haven of rest, but have become a place filled with selfish and abusive parents. Hence, many of our children are running away from home. Many youths that are turning to violence have behavioral problems—they kill their teachers and peers. They are a threat to society.

Is there hope for our children? Will we be able to correct the state of affairs in our homes, schools, churches, and society in general? The answer to both questions is *yes*! When love is returned to our homes, when the government allows parents to be parents, and when God is once again placed back in our schools, then there will be hope. As parents, we do not need to wait on the government for permission to be parents. We have received guidance from the Word of God. If we as parents demonstrate love toward each other and lovingly lead our children, our world will be a better place.

Paul Conn, in his book *Dad, Mom and the Church*, said:

Parents are many things for their children: providers, teachers, givers of emotional support, disciplinarians, chauffeurs, homework tutors, cheerleaders, and night watchmen, but most of all they are role models. Fathers are many things to their children, and one of the best gifts they can give to their children is to give love to their mothers. This provides hope and confidence that they would not have to fear separation, divorce, (or) living in a single-parent home except through death.[4]

When husbands demonstrate love to their wives, it sends a message to the children that amidst the stress, burden, and strain of life, love will cover a multitude of sins. Children will learn love is the key to a healthy relationship.

Dorothy Law Nolte expresses, in a lovely poem in her book, *Children Learn What They Live*, what children learn from the environment in which they live.[5]

## CHILDREN LEARN WHAT THEY LIVE

If a child lives with criticism, he learns to condemn.
If a child lives with hostility, he learns to fight.
If a child lives with fear, he learns to be apprehensive.
If a child lives with pity, he learns to feel sorry for himself.
If a child lives with ridicule, he learns to be shy.
If a child lives with jealousy, he learns what is envy.
If a child lives with shame, he learns to feel guilty.
If a child lives with encouragement, he learns to
    be confident.
If a child lives with tolerance, he learns to be patient.
If a child lives with praise, he learns to be appreciative.
If a child lives with acceptance, he learns to love.
If a child lives with approval, he learns to like himself.
If a child lives with recognition, he learns it is good to have
    a goal.
If a child lives with sharing, he learns about generosity.
If a child lives with honesty and fairness, he learns what
    truth and justice are.
If a child lives with security, he learns to have faith in himself and in those about him.

> If a child lives with friendliness, he learns that the world is
> a nice place in which to live.
> If you live with serenity, your child will live with peace of
> mind.

Many children are living in fear of divorce because their parents do not show love to each other. When love is missing between a husband and wife, in due time, separation or divorce will become a reality and this becomes a child's worse nightmare.

The problem we have in society today is we have bought the idea unhappy people should not have to stay in unhappy marriages. Our tolerant church and culture have given authority to couples to leave their marriages to change partners without any remorse when trouble comes.

Divorce has become a big business for lawyers. It is marketed in every media as a fast, affordable, and easy thing to do.

There are fifteen states that allow no-fault divorce. The No-Fault divorce allows any spouse to sue for divorce without having to prove that the other spouse did something wrong. All states allow divorces regardless of who is at "fault." However, to get a No-Fault divorce, one spouse must simply state a reason recognized by the state. In most states, it's enough to declare that the couple cannot get along. (This reason goes by such names as "incompatibility," "irreconcilable differences," or "irremediable breakdown of the marriage.")

In nearly a dozen states, however, the couple must live apart for a period of months or even years in order to obtain a no-fault divorce.

The truth is that the way couples are living with each other must be changed. Rather than getting rid of the spouse and keeping the problem, they should get rid of the problem and keep the partner.

Healthy marriages provide the feeling of necessity, that amidst difficulties couples will not run away from the problems of life, but will face them head on. That necessity creeps into the relationship at the first sign of trouble and becomes essential to one's feeling of safety and survival. Hence the saying, "I cannot imagine what it would be like, to be without you in my life." When each spouse realizes the necessity for the other in marriage, they will seek to create an environment to produce the lifelong rewards of happiness.

How can a couple create an environment of happiness in marriage? First they must trust in God, obey His words, and allow His love to permeate their every being. Gerald Anst, writing in the November/December 2003 issue of *The Good News Magazine,* said, "There is a seamless connection between God's commandments and true love."[5] Love is the central nervous system of every family and should be the ultimate goal in obtaining a healthy, sturdy, and happy family.

Let me pause here to directly address women. Before you enter into a relationship, be sure the man loves you as a whole person. Be sure he loves you for yourself, not for your possessions or outward beauty. All those things will change with time. Marriage will not change who you are. Instead, it will enhance or complete you. If the husband enters the relationship with the right attitude, respect, commitment, and knowledge, love will only get better with time and anything else will wane. First Corinthians 13:13 says, "And now these three remain: faith, hope and love. But the greatest of these is love." The verse is referring to spiritual things such as tongues, knowledge, and prophesying which will pass away, but faith, hope, and love will never pass away.

Everything in marriage will change, but love is the only constant since the husband is the head of the home and his role is modeled after the role of Christ as Head of the church, who "...loved the church and gave himself up for her" (Eph. 5:25). King Solomon tells us, in his commentaries on love, not even the grave can conquer it. (See Song of Solomon 8:6–7.) Love will follow us to our graves, and it will continue in the hearts of our spouses and children. For that reason it behooves us to continue giving love, because it will last through eternity.

Finally, I would like to share with you some information taken from Glenn Stanton, in his book, *Why Marriage Matters.*[6] Stanton said from all his research, he has determined that loving heterosexual married couples win out over every other type of family. The rewards and benefits of marriage are more satisfactory and fulfilling than any other arrangement. He highlights some of the benefits and rewards of marriage in the following list:

1. Most happy, healthy, safe, sexually fulfilled, and productive people are found among the married.

2. Men and women who are married do markedly better
   in all measures of specific and general well-being,
   compared to any of their unmarried counterparts.

3. Married couples are healthier psychologically. They
   live longer, enjoy a more fulfilled life, and take better
   care of themselves and each other.

4. Marriage provides genuine emotional and physical
   protection from myriad pressures and affliction of day-
   to-day life.

5. Seventy percent of divorced and separated people are
   alcoholics against 15 percent of married couples.

6. The highest suicide rates occur among the divorced,
   the widowed, and the never married, while it is the
   lowest among the married. Divorced individuals are
   three times more likely to commit suicide than those
   who are married.

7. Married people suffer less from illness and disease and
   typically enjoy a longer life than those who are not
   married.

8. Older married couples have invested themselves in a
   lifelong relationship, and they are reaping the benefits
   in contentment, companionship, and good health.
   Their love is bringing forth a harvest of benefits with
   each new year.

9. A loving marital relationship may reduce exposure to
   stress and provide a source of support during difficult
   times.

10. Cohabitating couples were more than twice as likely to
    suffer from any mental illness than a loving, married
    couple.

11. No part of the unmarried population—separated, di-
    vorced, widowed, or never married—describes itself as
    being so happy and contended with life as the married.

12. Loving, married couples are better workers, less likely to miss work, more productive on the job, more likely to stay employed for longer periods of time, and are more likely to get along with those with whom they work than unmarried coworkers.

13. The safest and healthiest child is one who grows up in a loving family.

Beyond a shadow of doubt, a loving marriage is the key to the survival of life on earth. So, as married people, we need to do all we can to build healthy and loving marriages to prolong the quality of life. You and I cannot do anything to change other lives and make it better or worse, but we have the power in us to change our marriage for the better. For those of us who are in the ministry, we owe it to our members and parishioners, as well as having an obligation by God's Word to preach and teach on the *Love Factor in Marriage* as much as we preach on the other issues in the Bible.

## DISCUSSION

1. How can parents demonstrate their love language to their children?

2. Why are so many families starving for love? How can that affect our children?

3. In what ways do husbands work from a logical point of view?

4. In what ways do women work from an emotional point of view?

5. What are some of the benefits of a loving marriage relationship?

6. How involved is God in your marriage?

7. Do you see your marriage providing any of the benefits listed?

8. What can you do to ensure your marriage will produce a loving heritage?

*Chapter 13*

# LOVING YOU FOREVER

*Set me as a seal upon thine heart, as a seal upon thine arm;*
*for love is strong as death; jealousy is cruel as the grave; the*
*coals thereof are coals of fire, which hath a most vehement*
*flame.*
—SONG OF SOLOMON 8:6, KJV

Is IT POSSIBLE to love one's wife or husband forever? Can true love last for a lifetime? Yes! Yes! Love is created to last as long as one is alive. Death is the only thing that can truly end love.

I do believe that God made man to love forever, but sin and a faulty socialization have marred human relationships and created a chemical dysfunction.

It seems scientists are cracking the genetic code to the infidelity problem. This is good news. According to an article in a South African daily newspaper, "In a remarkable experiment in hormone chemistry, behavioral scientists implanted a single gene into promiscuous male voles, transforming them at a stroke into faithful, attentive and caring partners."[1] Scientists believe that this discovery will lead to a cure for human infidelity. The Bible has a better cure. The indwelling present of the Holy Spirit will change the desire and nature of the adulterer if he or she would fully submit to Him.

Infidelity is one of the leading causes of divorce among Christians. Glenn Stanton, in his book, *Why Marriage Matters,* said "the United States of America is a divorcing culture."[2] Christian couples can turn the tide by learning how to show more love to their spouses. Learning to communicate love will ultimately lead to a lower divorce rate, happier homes, and a better society as a whole.

"I will love you forever" is probably the oldest expression ever used between lovers. That statement was, and still is, like music to the ears of those who receive it. However, today one wonders at the meaning of those words. The question that should be asked in response to that statement is, how long is forever? Is it until the "in-love" nostalgic feeling dies? Is it until we grow apart? Or is it until we find some irreconcilable difference?

These words, *I will love you forever*, are a vow to the receiver and a conscious choice made as part of a Christian marriage vow. "I will forsake all others…I will love you forever…until death do us part" were words most couples repeated to each other on their wedding day.

You may have thought those words were just part of a contract; however, those words were registered in heaven in a covenant witnessed by God himself according to Malachi's description of the marriage of Israel:

> You ask, 'Why?' It is because the LORD is acting as the witness between you and the wife of your youth, because you have broken faith with her, though she is your partner, the wife of your marriage covenant.
> —MALACHI 2:14

God expects husbands and wives to honor their marriage covenant to love each other forever.

Individuals usually remember when he or she falls in love. He or she met someone whose physical characteristics and personality traits created enough electrical current to trigger their "love-alert" system. The bells rang, the fireworks went off, and the process of getting to know the woman or man was set into motion. A few months or years later, the euphoric feelings waned, and they said the love tank was empty. The initial attraction was not as potent as it had been.

Many people enter their marriage union with the euphoric experience of falling in love. In his book, *The Five Love Languages*, Dr. Gary Chapman mentions that Dorothy Tennov, a psychologist who has done long-range study on the "in-love" phenomenon, indicates the average life span of a romantic obsession is two years.[3] When love wanes, many couples want to know what happened to that "in-love" feeling? Was it real? Yes, those feelings were real. So, what is the problem? Those feelings were coupled with faulty information that the euphoria would last forever.

Others consider falling in love to be unreal. One such person is Dr. M. Scott Peck. He gives three reasons why the falling-in-love feelings are not real in his book, *The Road Less Traveled*. "Falling in love is not an act of the will or a conscious choice; it is not real because it is effortless. The one who is in love is not genuinely interested in fostering the personal growth of the other person."

Dr. Hendrix adds, *In Keeping the Love You Find*:

> By falling madly in love with someone who has both the positive and the negative traits of our imperfect parents, someone who fits an image that we carry deep inside us, and for whose embodiment we see unconsciously searching. The Imago bond or falling in love creates a spurious wholeness.[4]

The problem with that view is that the attempt to get, through someone else, what is missing in ourselves never works, for personal emptiness cannot be filled by a partner.

Dr. Hendrix further adds:

> When we meet an Imago match, that chemical reaction occurs and love ignites. When we fall in love, we reawaken memories of that idyllic state of connection and joy with which we have lost contact. Memories of our original wholeness and essential connectedness come flooding back to us, and we credit our awakened aliveness to our beloved. It is he or she who makes us feel like dancing, *she* who inspires us to poetry, who is responsible for our loving the world, for our snapping out of boredom or depression or anger.

There are countless testimonies of marriages that start with individuals falling in love that are still happily married today; so there must be a level of realism to falling in love. However, there are many couples that start with the in-love feeling, and they never stop to think through the reason why their "love tanks" are empty. They continue to live in their misery or they divorce. Neither of those choices are the answer.

Love is a choice. And if a couple makes a commitment to love forever, there must be another alternative to pursue real love. In his book, *The Five Love Languages*, Dr. Chapman said:

> Our most basic need is not to fall in love, but to be genu-
> inely loved by another, to know a love that grows out of
> reason and choice, not instinct... That kind of love requires
> effort and discipline. One of the main reasons for ineffec-
> tive love communication is there is seldom the same love
> language communicated between husbands and wives.

The Christian marriage is not merely a contract between two people. It is a covenant that can only be nullified by death or by God. Therefore, when a couple enters into a Christian marriage and makes a vow to love forever, God holds them accountable to their obligations. The problem in many marriages is the lack of healthy and full "love tanks." Dr. Gary Chapman states there are five emotional love languages people speak and understand. I will address these love languages later in the chapter. However, there are unlimited ways to express love within a love language. The important thing is to be able to communicate the love lan-guage of your spouse. If husbands and wives would learn to speak each other's love language, then they would see an increase in their "love tanks" and a decline in the divorce rate.

The Barna Research Group interviewed nearly four thousand adults and found that "Christians are more likely to experience divorce than are non-Christians."[5] The data showed that although only 11 percent of the adult population is currently divorced, 25 percent of all adults have experienced at least one divorce during their lifetime. "Among born-again Christians, 27 percent are cur-rently or have previously been divorced; conversely, the total for non-Christians was 24 percent." That is a sad revelation.

Barna states:

> These findings were both expected and surprising. The
> national statistics have remained the same for the past half-
> decade. While it may be alarming to discover that born-
> again Christians are more likely than others to experience a
> divorce, that pattern has been in place for quite some time.

David Crary, a journalist writing for *The Associated Press* further adds to the divorce saga:

> Aside from the quickie-divorce mecca of Nevada, no region of the United States has a higher divorce rate than the following states in the Bible belt—Tennessee, Arkansas, Alabama, and Oklahoma. In a country where nearly half of all new marriages break up, the divorce rates in those conservative states are roughly 50 percent above national averages.[6]

Because it is so easy to get a divorce, many people use it as a way out of their marriage rather than trying to repair what is wrong. Many people do not believe it is too easy to get a divorce, but that it is too easy to get married. All one needs is twenty dollars and a blood test. Those who perform marriages are given permission to marry anyone who wants to be married. Then after marriage, newlyweds seem to think once they get into the first fight, the marriage is not going to work and the perfect person is waiting for them in the next marriage. There is no attitude of "sticking with it" and trying to work out the problems. Divorce is not the only choice. There is a better way.

Some denominations are encouraging clergy to marry only those couples that first take a marriage preparation course. That is a good beginning. However, I think just as people are required by law to study the driver's handbook and practice their driving skills before they are granted a license to drive, a similar requirement should be implemented by the government or the church, requiring individuals wanting to get married to go through a preparation course. There are politicians who are busily working to implement measures aimed at cutting the divorce rate in half.

Many churches are spearheading initiatives to promote marriage preparation. Among the possibilities of correcting the divorce dilemma, couples are encouraged to accept mediation before considering divorce. Courses are offered in public schools that deal with values and relationships. This is good news for marriage. However, what I would consider a great help for marriage and family education would be the return of prayer and

God in the public school. It is good to introduce courses that will teach values in school, but any course designed to teach the absolute in values that is void of God will be flawed. Education and legislation will help to decrease the divorce rate, but the true answer to divorce is in a rekindled love relationship.

If husbands and wives would learn each other's love languages and practice them, their homes would be filled with happiness. Wives—this is what God is calling husbands to do. God wants husbands to learn their wives' love languages and to communicate by using them. It is the responsibility of the husband, as the leader, to take the initiative. Meeting his wife's needs for love is a choice the husband must make daily. When husbands speak their wives' love languages every day, they will meet their wives' deepest emotional needs, and wives will feel secure in the love their husbands give. When husbands lead in love, it is easier for wives to reciprocate—submit to love, reverence, and respect.

Christian marriages should begin with mutual love and obedience to the Word of God. When couples allow their "love tanks" to go empty for a long time it may lead to abuse and finally divorce. "I will love you forever" is a choice and a conscious commitment one makes. Therefore, if, in the process of time, husbands and wives see that their "love tanks" begin to empty, they need to find out the reason for the depletion and try to restore that love.

If one makes the right choice to give love a chance, to work and heal the love-starved marriage relationship, then love will prevail. It begins with the "right attitude and way of thinking," said Dr. Chapman in his book *The Five Love Languages*. Here are the five love languages that Dr. Chapman lists as ways of communicating love in a marriage:

1. Words of affirmation

2. Quality time

3. Receiving gifts

4. Acts of service

5. Physical touch

Many husbands and wives complain about showing love to their spouses, because it is never appreciated. Generally speaking, people usually show appreciation for things they receive. Therefore, wives will show appreciation for love if it is given through the proper channel or expression, in their love language. Some men may be showering their wives with gifts or helping with the house chores as a means of expressing their love, but the wives may not be showing positive responses of appreciation. If a woman's number one love language is quality time, she will respond with greater love and appreciation when she is given quality time.

If a husband expresses his love through the wrong love language, it will not produce the ecstasy, thrill, and love his wife expects. Gift giving, acts of service, quality time, and touching will be appreciated and accepted when your spouse feels fully loved and affirmed. Loving your spouse forever must be governed by loving principles. In the following question taken from his book, *Keeping the Love You Find*, Dr. Hendrix asks about the basis for real love. He outlines ten principles a couple should follow to make their love last forever.

What does a relationship, based on real love—a *conscious* relationship—look like?

1. *The basic principle of a conscious relationship is intentionality.* The partners in a conscious relationship recognize the purpose of their relationship is to heal their wounds. They are committed to identifying the drives and directives of their unconscious and to designing their relationship to cooperate with them. They recognize their partners' need is a blueprint for their own personal growth. They realize following this blueprint will involve arduous work, and they must be committed to the process.

2. *In a conscious relationship, partners exchange unconditional gifts.* The partners in a conscious relationship educate each other about their wounds. They identify their partners' needs and desires, and they commit

themselves to meeting them unconditionally. They take inspiration from the romantic-low stage of their relationship and offer their partners unconditional love. That is, they specifically target their behavior to meet their partners' needs and heal their wounds, without asking for anything in return.

3. *In a conscious relationship, partners are separate, but equal.* Partners in a conscious relationship accept each other with absolute separateness. By their unique way of perceiving reality, and the sacredness of each other's inner worlds, they consider themselves equals. They explore and mirror each other's worlds, validate each other's experience, and empathize with each other's feelings.

4. *In a conscious relationship, there are no exits.* The partners in a conscious relationship keep all the energy that belongs in the relationship within its bounds. When they feel uncomfortable or when their needs are not being met, they bring their concerns to their partner rather than withdrawing from the relationship or getting their needs met outside the relationship. Rather than acting out, they convert their feelings into constructive communication.

5. *In a conscious relationship, there is no criticism.* The partners in a conscious relationship communicate their needs and desires to each other in constructive ways. They do not criticize or blame each other, and they do not use provocation or coercion to try to get their partners to fulfill those needs and desires.

6. *In a conscious relationship, anger is expressed by appointment only.* The partners in a conscious relationship accept all of each other's feelings, especially anger. They realize anger is an expression of pain, and that pain usually has its roots in an unresolved issue. Conscious partners never express anger or frustration spontaneously, for they know "dumping" negative feelings is destructive. They learn constructive ways of containing and expressing anger and other negative

emotions, and they help their partner do so in non-judgmental ways as well. Expressing their anger in a contained way leads to its conversion into passion and deeper bonding.

7. *In a conscious relationship, both partners are responsible for and carry all aspects of themselves.* The partners in a conscious relationship learn to own their own negative traits instead of projecting them onto, and provoking them, in their partner. They accept responsibility for those parts of themselves of which they are not proud, and learn to manage and integrate them.

8. *In a conscious relationship, each partner calls the other to wholeness.* The partners in a conscious relationship develop their own lost strengths and abilities instead of relying on their partner to make up for what is missing or lost in themselves. They are, therefore, more whole, and they foster wholeness in their partners.

9. *In a conscious relationship, each partner strives for androgyny.* The partners in a conscious relationship develop their own supra-sexual energy and encourage the development of their partner's supra-sexual energy. They do not behave or expect their partners to behave in accordance with culture, gender, or sexual stereotypes. They share income responsibilities as well as household responsibilities, chores, and child care in accordance with each partner's interests, abilities, and schedules, rather than a code of social expectations.

10. *In a conscious relationship, partners care for each other and their environment.* The partners in a conscious relationship are whole and balanced and in touch with their sense of oneness with the environment in which they live. Each partner creates the environment that allows each other the opportunity to grow, and mature within themselves, and as a couple.

Dr. Horace Ward, former senior pastor of South Cleveland Church of God in Cleveland, Tennessee, presented another way couples can build their love lives when he addressed his church's lay ministry breakfast one morning. He said, "There are seven key ingredients to restore and maintain a great love life or to keep the sparkle in the your love life." They are:

1. Commitment
2. Companionship
3. Considerateness
4. Care
5. Communication
6. Compassion
7. Consummation

After listening to the address, I reflected on the five different types of love. I realized the above list, when properly applied, would supply all the different types of love. Agape love is unconditional love and such love requires commitment in order for it to truly function. Eros love, which is romantic love, requires considerateness in providing the romantic needs of each mate. Phileo love is expressed through friendship, and it takes genuine companionship to provide a good friendship. Storge love is expressed in the feeling of belonging and requires care when reaching out to meet such needs. Finally, epithumia love, which is lovemaking, is the physical way God designed husbands and wives to consummate their love.

Happy heterosexual marriages are financial assets to a strong society. As a result, many governments are now spending billions of dollars to build the quality of marriage and minimize the divorce epidemic.

The question is, what can we do to strengthen, maintain, and uphold loving relationships in marriages today? We must first make a commitment or recommitment that we will be true to our marriage vows, "for better for worse…in sickness and in health, until death us do part." For too long the marriage commitment has been treated more like a contract rather than a divine covenant, which can only be nullified by death. Couples entering marriage need to take time to be counseled about the sacredness of marriage and what taking the vows entails. When Spirit-filled Christians take the marriage vows, they are not taking it alone. The Holy Spirit's presence gives them the power to be witnesses to a loving marriage until death. The Holy Spirit never leaves the marriage. He always there to aide each spouse in their lives to the maximum.

A Spirit-filled heterosexual marriage is the safest place for growth, longevity, happiness, health, and wealth. But, too many people are running away from problems rather than fixing them. Problems cannot be solved by running—it will only follow. If your marriage is in trouble, your love is wounded, and there is no intimacy; seek God's help. He has the solution for your problems, but you must be willing to submit completely to His will and words.

Build companionship between each other, so nothing will separate you from each other. People like to spend time with friends. Create in your schedule things you can do together and spend quality time to build your friendship. Working together will build a bond and friendship that will forge oneness and will keep out marriage killers.

Be considerate. Live your life to include the feelings of your spouse. Whatever you do, think of how it will benefit the whole, not just you. You are in a partnership, so whatever you do should be done with consideration for the other person's feelings and growth.

Be very caring. Kindness is the way in which you demonstrate your love for your spouse by your thoughts and actions. The kind things you do will affirm the worth, value, respect, and love for your spouse. Be gentle to each other.

Take time to communicate. One of the major problems in marriage is lack of communication. Many people enter marriage feeling that once they are married, their spouse will be able to fully understand their thoughts and feelings without proper communication. Unmet expectations are many times the result of lack of communication. The only way to avoid expectation dilemmas is to communicate what is expected. No one can read another person's mind. Take time to talk and share all your feelings, so your partner will be able to do the things that please you and make you happy.

Be compassionate. Endeavor to be sympathetic, kindhearted, and empathetic to your partner. Walking in the shoes of your partner minimizes marital conflicts and produces a greater appreciation for their worth.

Make time to consummate your marriage. Too many people are so busy they do not make quality time to consummate their love. Sex is not an addendum to marriage, it is a litmus test of your love. Sexual activities express the true intimacy and oneness of marriage. It is an integral part of every marriage. It was not given as an afterthought of God, and it was given to the marriage for pleasure, procreation, and oneness. The more sex is lovingly shared in marriage, it is symbolizing the oneness of the marriage. Sex is a holy gift given by God only to be expressed in marriage. According to Linda Dillow and Lorraine Pintus, in their book *Intimate Issues*, God gave us sex to "create life, pleasure, knowledge, bonding, intimate oneness, as defense against temptation and for comfort."[7]

Age in marriage does not limit the quality or quantity of lovemaking. It is a gift of God and married partners must seek ways guided by biblical principles in keeping their sex lives alive so they can experience Gods' love, as it can only be experienced through sexual intercourse. Many believers and ministers are falling into sexual sins and ultimately destroying their marriages and ministries because they fail to grow sexually in their marriage.

The Christian church has ignored marriage and family for too long. As a result, we have seen a breakdown and decay in the families and marriages of the church. God thought so highly of marriage that when he described the relationship of Jesus Christ and the church, he used it as an illustration in Ephesians 5:21–37. We do not have the power to stop legal maneuvering of the redefinition of marriage, but we have the power to improve our love dynamics, marriages, and families.

In the areas Dr. Ward listed, there must be a passion to communicate clearly and concisely in each type of love so the marriage will grow and become sweeter with each passing day.

Love will either grow or die by how husbands and wives handle it in a relationship. If a couple applies Dr. Ward's formula, guided by the indwelling presence of the Holy Spirit, love will grow. The apostle Paul charged husbands to love their wives and charged wives to submit to their husbands. He charged them both to be completely filled and to be continuously filled with the Spirit of God rather than being filled with the spirit that leads to debauchery. (See Ephesians 5:18.) A person who is Spirit-filled will express love for his or her spouse. The Holy Spirit will teach that individual how to love.

One of the problems we face today is many believers are filled with the wrong spirit. Many of our churches in North America seem to be filled with the spirit of the world where marriage is concerned. When the Holy Spirit controls our lives, we will love our spouses the way God intended. However, when other spirits influence our lives, we will not have the necessary power to handle the difficulties and stresses of marital relationships. Ultimately, we will be tempted to neglect nurturing love.

If your "love tank" seems to be running dry or your feeling of love for your spouse seems to be dying, there is hope if the Holy Spirit still resides in you. Love is a choice you make. Christ chose to love us even while we were still sinners. His love gave us life. The choice we make to love our spouses is unconditional: "I will love you forever."

The *only* power that can separate love is God. Jesus said, about the marriage union in Matthew 19:6, "So they are no longer two, but one. Therefore what God has joined together, let man not separate."

The Greek word for *joined* is *proskollao,* which means to fasten together—to glue together, to cement together; to be joined in the closest union possible, to be bound together; to be so totally united that two become one. Therefore, to join means a spiritual union. It is a union higher and stronger than the union of parent and child. It is a union that means more than living together, more than having sex and bearing children. It is a spiritual fullness, a spiritual sharing of life together—dedication, consecration, completeness, satisfaction—that makes husbands and wives the exclusive possession of God and each other. God designed such a cleaving or spiritual union, and only God can dissolve the bond.

Three unions take place in a true marriage bond joined by God. They are the physical union, or the sharing of their bodies (see 1 Corinthians 7:2–5); the mental union, the sharing of their lives, hopes, and dreams, working together to realize them; and, the spiritual union, the sharing, melding, and molding of their spirits. (See Ephesians 5:25–33.) Those unions are designed to grow daily as they are watered in love.

Let us not forget God is the author of love, and He is the One who works the "joining." If He dwells in you, He will provide you with the necessary grace to live with situations that are sometimes unpleasant or will provide a way to overcome and solve the problem. There are many good books on the market that can help Christian marriages. If the God of love resides in you, He is willing to provide the necessary love you need to cause your marriage love bonds to grow and mature with time and age. If you will genuinely seek His help, you will receive it today.

God has never commanded, and will never command, His children to do the impossible without making it possible. So, if you are in need of love healing, restoration in your marriage, or if your family is hurting and your world seems to be falling apart, let me encourage you to begin afresh by inviting the God of love in to heal and restore your love for your spouse.

## DISCUSSION

1. When you told your spouse "I will love you forever," what did those words really mean to you? Do they mean the same today?

2. Why do you think so many young couples do not take their marriage vows seriously?

3. Do you know your love language? Does your mate know your love language?

4. Discuss your love language with your mate. Share ways you intend to nurture each other using your love languages.

# CONCLUSION

Now that you have read the book and gained some new insight about your love responsibilities, communicate with your husband or wife. Ask questions. Find out what his or her love language is. Develop a habit of practicing your spouse's love language. Restore your love, grow in love, and, if needed, seek qualified pastoral marital counseling to help maintain your revived love. Above all else, pray! The God of love can bring you and your spouse together, and you will be able to say, "Beloved, if God so loved us, we ought also to love one another" (1 John 4:11, KJV).

If you and your spouse have begun to use the suggestions mentioned in this book, I believe you are ready to rebuild and enrich your love relationship. My prayer is that each day you will turn to God for guidance in your marriage. He will teach you how to love, and He will guide you in that love, because He is love.

## WAYS TO ENHANCE ROMANCE

Here are some suggestions given by Dr. Wayne Mack in his book, *Homework Manual for Biblical Counseling*, which can be used to improve your love life.[1]

## WAYS A HUSBAND CAN EXPRESS LOVE TO HIS WIFE

Husbands need to evaluate the ways they express love to their wives daily. Listed below are some ways to demonstrate your love. Go over the list and circle the ways you may be neglecting to

154

show love to your wife. Ask your wife to go over the list and put a check mark in front of the ways she would like you to express love. Ask her to add other ways to the list. Here are some ways to demonstrate your love:

1. Function as the loving leader of your home.

2. Frequently tell her you love her.

3. If she does not work outside the home, give her an agreed-upon amount of money to spend any way she chooses.

4. Lead family devotions regularly.

5. Do something spontaneous and zany—do not always be predictable.

6. Share the household chores.

7. Take care of the children for at least three hours every week so she has free time to do whatever she wants.

8. Take her out for dinner or do something fun at least once a week.

9. Do the "fix-it" jobs she wants done around the house.

10. Greet her when you come home with a smile, a hug, a kiss, and an "I am glad to see you. I really missed you today."

11. Give her a lingering kiss.

12. Pat her on the shoulder, hold her hand, and caress her frequently.

13. Be willing to talk to her about her concerns and do not belittle her for having them.

14. Look at her with an adoring expression.

15. Sit close to her.

16. Rub her back.

17. Shave, take a bath, and brush your teeth before you have sexual relations.

18. Wear her favorite aftershave.

19. Write love notes or letters to her.

20. Let her know you appreciate her and what you appreciate

about her. Do that often and for things that are sometimes taken for granted.

21. Fulfill her implied or unspoken wishes as well as the specific requests she make of you.

22. Anticipate what she might like and surprise her by doing it before she asks.

23. Play together, share her hobbies and recreational preferences enthusiastically, and include her in yours.

24. Set a good example before the children.

25. Talk about her favorably to the children when she can hear you, and even when she cannot.

26. Brag about her good points to others; let her know you are proud to have her as your wife.

27. Maintain your own spiritual life through Bible study, prayer, regular church attendance, and fellowship with God's people.

28. Structure your time and use it wisely; be on time to go places.

29. Make plans prayerfully and carefully.

30. Ask her advice when you have a problem or decisions to make.

31. Follow her advice unless to do so would violate biblical principles.

32. Fulfill your responsibilities.

33. Be sober, but not somber, about life.

34. Have a realistic, biblical, positive attitude toward life.

35. Discuss plans with your wife before you make decisions, and when the plans are made, share them fully with your wife, giving reasons for the decisions you made.

36. Thank her in creative ways for her attempts to please you.

37. Ask forgiveness often, and say, "I was wrong and will try to change."

38. Actually change areas of your life that you know need changing.

39. Share your insights and good experiences with her.

40. Plan a mini-honeymoon.

41. Give some expression of admiration when she wears a new dress or your favorite negligee.

42. Gently brush her leg under the table.

43. Be reasonably happy to go shopping with her.

44. Relate what happened at work or whatever you did apart from her.

45. Reminisce about the early days of your marriage.

## Ways a Wife Can Express Love to Her Husband

Evaluate the way you express your love to your husband. Go over the list and circle any ways you may be neglecting to show love for your husband. Ask your husband to go over the list and put a check mark in front of the ways he would like you to express love. Ask him to add other things to the list.

1. Greet him at the door when he comes home with a smile, a hug, a kiss, and an "I am glad to see you! I really missed you today."

2. Have a cup of coffee or tea ready for him when he comes home from work or a trip.

3. Give him a lingering kiss.

4. Let him know you like being with him and make arrangements so you can spend time with him without giving the impression you really should or would rather be doing something else.

5. Be willing to talk to him about his concerns without belittling him for having those concerns.

6. Support him and cooperate with him enthusiastically when he has made a decision.

7. Tease and flirt with him.

8. Seek to arouse him, and sometimes be the aggressor in sexual relations.

9. Ask him to have sexual relations more than he would expect you to.

10. Express yourself passionately during sexual relations.

11. Caress him.

12. Look at him with an adoring expression.

13. Sit close to him.

14. Hold his hand.

15. Rub his back.

16. Wear his favorite nightgown, dress, or perfume.

17. Express your love in words or notes.

18. Let him know you appreciate him and what you appreciate about him.

19. Do that often and for things that are sometimes taken for granted.

20. Frequently fulfill his unspoken wishes as well as the specific requests he makes of you. Try to anticipate what he might like and surprise him by doing it before he asks.

21. Play together; for example, tennis, golf, or party games, among others.

22. Enthusiastically share with him in devotions and prayer; seek to set a good example for the children concerning their attitudes toward devotions and prayer.

23. Maintain your own spiritual life through Bible study and prayer.

24. Structure your time and use it wisely.

25. Be willing to face and solve problems even if it requires discomfort, change, and much effort.

26. Fulfill your responsibilities.

27. Ask him for his advice and frequently follow it.

28. Be ready to leave at the appointed time.

29. Stand with him and support him in his attempts to raise your children for God.

30. Thank him in creative ways for his attempts to please you.

31. Ask for forgiveness by saying, "I was wrong and will try to change."

32. Actually change areas of your life that you know need changing.

33. Work with him on his projects.

34. Read books or magazine articles he asks you to read and share your insights.

35. Let him know, when he has to make a decision, you believe he will make the right choice and you wholeheartedly support him in whatever choice he makes, provided the decision does not clearly violate revealed biblical principles.

36. Be his best cheerleader and fan.

37. Buy gifts for him.

38. Show genuine interest in his hobbies.

    a. Watch or attend sporting events with him.

    b. Listen to him sing and play the guitar or piano.

    c. Attend a class he teaches.

39. Keep the house neat and clean.

40. Cook creative, nutritious meals, or praise him when he does.

41. Have devotions with the children when he is not able to be there.

42. Maintain his disciplinary rules when he is not present.

43. Be cooperative and appreciative when he holds you, caresses you, or kisses you.

44. Lovingly give him your input when you think he is in error.

45. Offer constructive suggestions when you think he could improve or become more productive. Do not push, preach, or do it in a way you belittle him; instead seek nonthreatening ways to help him become the man God wants him to be.

There are many ways to express love to your spouse. Since people express and experience love in different ways, take time to share with each other how you can show love. Only you and your spouse know your true feelings—love languages—so talk about what will satisfy the love needs you both have and do your best to cultivate those needs.

# NOTES

## Chapter 1
### THE LOVE FACTOR IGNITE

1. Harville Hendrix, PhD, *Keeping the Love You Find* (New York: Pocket Book, 1992).
2. Ibid.
3. Ibid.
4. Ibid.
5. Ibid.
6. Ibid.
7. Helen Fisher, PhD, *Anatomy of Love* (New York: Ballantine Books, 1992).
8. Barbara DeAngelis, PhD, *Are You the One for Me?* (New York: Dell Publishing Company, 1993).
9. Ibid.

## Chapter 2
### THE LOVE BUNDLE

1. Willard J. Harley Jr., *Fall in Love and Stay in Love* (Grand Rapids, MI: Fleming H. Revell Co., 2001).

2. Hendrix, *Keeping the Love You Find.*

3. Willard J. Harley Jr., *Love Busters* (Grand Rapids, MI: Fleming H. Revell Co., 2002).

4. Adapted from http://www.marriagebuilders.com (accessed 2/19/04).

## Chapter 3
### ECSTASY RESTORED

1. Robert F. Stahmann and William J Hiebert, *Premarital and Remarital Counseling* (San Francisco: Jossey-Bass, 1997).

2. Thomas Bradbury, *The Development Course of Marital Dysfunction* (New York: Cambridge University Press, 1998).

## Chapter 4
### THE LOVING THING TO DO

1. Cable News Network (CNN), news report, October 1997.
2. Jim Shahin, "I Know What Love Is," *American Way*, February 2, 1999.
3. Harville Hendrix, PhD, *Keeping the Love You Find* (New York: Pocket Books, 1992).
4. Cynthia Heald, *Loving Your Husband* (Colorado Springs, CO: NavPress Publications, 1989).
5. American Broadcasting Corp., *20/20*, November 4, 1998.
6. Church of God Women's Ministry Deptartment, *Silent Suffering...Silent Shame* (Cleveland, TN: Pathway Press, 2000).
7. Willard J. Harley Jr., *His Needs, Her Needs* (Grand Rapids, MI: Fleming H. Revell Co., 2001).

## Chapter 7
### LOVING PARTNERSHIP

1. Matthew Henry, *Matthew Henry's Commentary*, Vol. 6 (Tappen, NJ: Fleming H. Revell).

2. Ibid.

## Chapter 8
### SILENCING LOVE

1. David Levinson, *Family Violence in Cross-Cultural Perspective* (London: Sage Publications, 1989).

2. Nancy Kilgore, *A Journey Through Domestic Violence Every Eighteen Seconds* (California: Volcano Press, 1992).

3. Rita-Lou Clarke, *Pastoral Care of Battered Women* (Philadelphia, PA: The Westminster Press, 1986).

4. Rollo May, *Power and Innocence* (New York: Fontana, 1979).

5. Lenore Walker, *The Battered Woman* (New York: Harper and Row, 1979).

6. Ann Storr, *Family Violence: An International and Interdisciplinary Study* (Toronto: Butterworth, 1978).

7. M. A. Allen and I. M. Allen, *Basics of Qualitative Research: Techniques and Procedures for Developing Grounded Theory,* 2nd edition (Thousand Oaks, CA: Sage Publications, 1998).

8. Ann Jones, *Next Time She'll Be Dead* (Boston: Beacon Press, 1994).

9. Jan Horsfall, *The Presence of the Past* (North Sydney, New South Wales, Australia: I. M. Allen and Unwin, 1991).

10. Marie Fortune, *Keeping the Faith* (San Francisco: Harper and Row 1987).

## Chapter 9
### KEEPING LOVE ALIVE IN THE STAGES OF MARRIAGE

1. Dr. Linda Waite and Maggie Gallagher, *The Case for Marriage* (New York: Doubleday, 1999).

2. Sharyn Wolf, *So You Want to Get Married* (New York: Dutton/Plume, 1999).

3. Jawanza Kamjufu, *Restoring the Village, Values, and Commitment: Solutions for the Black Family* (Chicago, IL: African American Images, 2001).

4. Less Parrott, *Relationship* (Grand Rapids, MI: Zondervan Press, 2002).

5. Harville Hendrix, PhD, *Keeping the Love You Find* (New York: Pocket Books, 1992).

## Chapter 10
### LOVE AND INTIMACY

1. Dr. Harry Schaumburg, *False Intimacy* (Colorado Springs, CO: NavPress, 2000).

2. Dr. Douglas Rosenau, *A Celebration of Sex* (Nashville, TN: Nelson/Word Pub. Group, 1994).

3. Terry Wier, *Holy Sex God's Purpose and Plan for Our Sexuality* (New

Kensington, PA: Whittaker House, 1999).

4. Willard J. Harley Jr., *Fall in Love and Stay in Love* (Grand Rapids, MI: Fleming H. Revell Co., 2001).

## Chapter 11
### LOVE AND SEX

1. Eric Fuchs, *Sexual Desire and Love* (New York: Seabury Press, 1983).

2. Mary Ann Mayo, *Christian Guide to Sexual Counseling* (Grand Rapids, MI: Zondervan, 1987).

3. Tim Stafford, *Sexual Chaos* (Downers Grove, IL: Intervarsity, 1993).

4. Terry Wier, *Holy Sex: God's Purpose and Plan for Our Sexuality* (New Kensington, PA: Whittaker House, 1999).

5. Taken from http://www.symptomtracker.com/page1138.htm, accessed 2/19/04.

6. Harville Hendrix, PhD, *Keeping the Love You Find* (New York: Pocket Book, 1992).

## Chapter 12
### LOVE'S REWARDS

1. Gary Chapman, PhD, *The Five Love Languages* (Chicago, IL: Northfield Publishing, 1995).

2. George Barna, Barna Research Group, www.Barna.org, (accessed December 21, 1999).

3. Charles Paul Conn, *Mom, Dad and the Church* (Cleveland, TN: Pathway Press, 1989).

4. Dorothy Law Nolte, Rachel Harris, and Jack Canfield, *Children Learn What They Live: Parenting to Inspire Values* (New York: Workman Publishing Company, 1998).

5. Gerald Anst, *The Good News Magazine,* Nov./Dec. 2003 issue, United Church of God International Association Press.

6. Glenn T. Stanton, *Why Marriage Matters* (Colorado Springs, CO: Pinon Press, 1997).

## Chapter 13
### LOVING YOU FOREVER

1. "Love Rat Could Spring Playboys A Fidelity Trap," *The Mercury*, Friday, June 18, 2004.

2. M. Scott Peck, PhD, *The Road Less Traveled* (New York: Simon and Schuster, 1978)

3. Gary Chapman, PhD, *The Five Love Languages* (Chicago, IL: Northfield Publishing, 1995).

4. Harville Hendrix, PhD, *Keeping the Love You Find* (New York: Pocket Book, 1992).

5. George Barna, Barna Research Group, www.Barna.org, (accessed December 21, 1999).

6. David Crary, *Wife Battering.* Associated Press Articles.

7. Linda Dillow, *Intimate Issues* (Colorado Springs, CO: WaterBrook Press, 1999).

## Conclusion

1. Wayne Mack, *A Homework Manual for Biblical Counseling*, vol. 2 (Phillipsburg, NJ: P & R Publishing Co., 1980). Used by permission.

# About the Author

Bishop Daniel J. Vassell Sr., a former teacher, pastor, and state youth and Christian education director, is now serving as a coordinator in the youth and Christian education department with the Church of God International offices in Cleveland, Tennessee.

Bishop Vassell is an internationally recognized speaker on marriage and family relationships. He is the author of *The Love Factor in Marriage*, first published in 2001, and has presented Love Factor seminars and conferences to thousands across the U.S., Canada, Europe, Africa, and the Caribbean. Daniel writes a monthly article on marriage and family issues for *Christian News Magazine*, published in Durban, South Africa.

Bishop Vassell is a graduate of Tyndale Seminary with a BRE degree. He majored in youth and Christian education. He also attended the Church of God Theological Seminary in Cleveland, Tennessee, where he earned a masters of arts degree in Christian counseling and currently is pursuing his doctorate in marriage and family counseling.

For speaking engagements, contact Bishop Vassell at Daniel@lovefactor.org, or if you need information on his ministry, go to www.lovefactor.org.

Bishop Vassell lives in Cleveland, Tennessee, with his wife, Jenny, and their two children, James and Aleah. Bishop Vassell enjoys reading, fishing, and, most of all, spending time with his family.